THE JOURNEY OF THE SOUL

WHAT HAPPENS WHEN YOU DIE?

OLIVIA AND RAF OCAÑA
5TH DIMENSION EARTH

First published by 5th Dimension Earth 2020.

Written by Olivia & Raf Ocaña.

Cover formatted by Helen Poole.

The right of Rafael and Olivia Ocaña to be identified as the authors of this work has been asserted by them in accordance with the Copyright, Designs and Patents Act 1988.

ISBN 978-1-9164029-5-9

CONTENTS

INTRODUCTION

The Journey Of The Soul has been Created because so many have been Asking. Asking to Know. Asking to Understand. Asking for Clarity. Asking for Help. One of the greatest Fears that Exist for so many is "what happens when I Die?". For some, this is a low hum of periodic Agitation, for others, it Creates a strong Fear that impacts their every day Life. So too are the Fears for those who have lost a Loved One. Someone who meant so much to them and yet, they Fear for where they are Now and if they will ever See them again.

The Journey Of The Soul is written to detail the in depth Understanding of Transition. For Transition is the Term covering the Process that occurs after the Death of a Physical Human, yet we also explain what comes before that Transition point and also what happens afterwards. For Death is the Outcome that results in the Physical Body of a Physical Human to no longer Be able to Live in The Physical Realm. Transition is how The Soul Moves from The Physical Realm to The Ethereal Realm to Become fully a

Non Physical Human. It should Be Understood that The Physical Realm References that which is 3rd Dimensional and where Physical Humans Live. The Ethereal Realm References that which is 4th Dimensional and above, and where Non Physical Humans and other Non Physical Energy Live.

Non Physical Humans are those Soul Energies that are commonly Understood as Angels, as spirit, Source Energy, or as ghosts even, yet there is so much more to Understand and demystify. For example, you have a Higher Self, every single Physical Human has one, and your Higher Self is a Non Physical Human Soul. So too is every Transitioned Loved One and they are accessible to you once you Understand more.

We Hope that in the Understanding of this Insight, that you Feel within your Soul a Connection, a Knowing, a Truth. We Hope you Enjoy Understanding brand new Insight around Ethereal Energy, around Creation, around your Soul Makeup and around Non Physical. That as you Go on to Create as a Physical Human in your Physical Life, that you Do so with a fullness of 'Who You Truly Are', Eternally. For so much of The Journey Of The Soul can Be Felt, Understood and Acted upon as you are Living your Physical Life.

How Do we Know?

With Transition, of course it is a challenging topic, for how Do you really Know unless you have Experienced it?

You are Taking this Opportunity to Understand. To Feel into all that is written in this book. We cannot convince you, for this is not what this book is about nor what we, 5th Dimension Earth are about. This book is about providing you with the Clarity, the

Insight, the Wonder of Transition and for you to Allow the Truth of this to Be Felt. If you Do, it will Create within you Love. It will Create within you Possibility and Connection and Hope. It will automatically Let Go Fear in relation to this topic and also any Fear that you have picked up along your Journey relating to those close to you who have Transitioned.

We Understand that many readers will have Existing Beliefs, some very Strong and inherited, others that were Formed based on their Experiences. We Know that this will challenge some of those Beliefs but Try to stay the course of the book. Try to Allow a new Perspective, for it may Create in you the very thing that you are looking for.

Spiritual References

You may have Noticed, even in this Introduction that there are capital letters where ordinarily there wouldn't Be. When there is a Spiritual Intention Protocol, Spiritual Intention, Spiritual Function, Spiritual Term or Spiritual Reference, then you will See this as a capitalised word, perhaps mid-sentence. This is not an editing mistake. This is in line with The New Language of Energy which 5th Dimension Earth is bringing forth at this Time. So much more to come on this in Future publications.

Know that Spiritual Intention Protocols Form the basis of All Creation. Energetically above these come Spiritual Term, an Energy that Forms part of Creation and links Spiritual Intention Protocols together with Knowing and Truth. Spiritual Function Flows Energetically above Spiritual Term and links with Energetic Law to Reference the most Important of Parameters for Life. All of these Form part of the umbrella that is Spiritual Reference. For there are many other words that you will Hear or See or Feel or

Know from us at 5th Dimension Earth that have a Spiritual Reference. These are more than words for they are of God, Precious and Ethereal.

Over Time we Hope that you will come to Use Spiritual References in your every day Life, for they are always in every part of it.

1

WHY YOU MATTER AND YOUR SOUL UNDERSTANDING

_____

YOUR LIFE IS WORTH LIVING

Take a moment. Pause. Look around. You Created this. Your scruffy dog drinking loudly from his bowl. That's you that is. Isn't Life wonderful Knowing you have around you a highly intelligent and Loving pet in your house that you nurture and walk and feed and play with and adore?

That keyboard that you have that keeps playing up on your laptop, irritating as it is, shouldn't keep you from the sheer Wonder of Knowing that 'Life Is Worth Living'. The Energy that you expend in complaining about your Life on Earth as a Physical Human Takes from your Soul in a way that is only Truly comprehended when you Transition.

Your Life Is Worth Living.

.   .   .

This simple sentence has more than an English language Definition, it also is Spiritual Reference. A Spiritual Reference that is Recorded within The 'Truth Of You', in your Soul, for every Human, Physical and Non Physical. A Spiritual Reference that drives us as Physical Humans to Connect to one of the most Precious Elements of our Soul...God.

For it is God that Created us, and alongside our Higher Selves, the two of them Designed us to individually Be many things but Importantly, with two common Aspects that are particular to all Human Souls. That is 'Self Love' and 'Acceptance of God's Destiny'. When these two Aspects are Triggered together, they Light Up your Soul Energy and Call 'The Truth Of You' in your Soul, and in Doing so your Conscious Mind Hears 'Your Life Is Worth Living'. It is these two Aspects together that also Unconsciously Connect us to a Knowing in our Soul that 'Life Is Worth Living'. A Highly evolved Physical Human can Unconsciously Feel this Knowing and with it comes a Sense of True, of Faith, of Trust, of Destiny and so to an Acceptance that God Created us to Live a Life of the most Unlimited Achievement. Boundless, Free, utterly Connected to ourselves, Nature and Humanness.

Your Life Is Worth Living.

This may not Be Felt by you as you read these words right Now but Know. Know that you have already Accepted this to Be True. Know that if you Allow it you will Consciously Remember this to Be True. These Times as we write this book are Precious, and this Means these Times are of God. More so than before, for in these Times he brings with him a Connection to Truth, Your Truth, His Truth. Do not Fear this or See this as a demand or proclamation from him. Simply See it as Love. Your Love, His Love. For Your Love and His Love are Aligned. Your Love and His Love are always together as one. No matter how far you stray from yourself, from God, this Understanding cannot Be undone.

God Created this wondrous planet called Earth for you to Co-Create in and to Live out an Existence of Truth that contains Joy, Fun, Ethereal Connection, a Connection to Nature and to simply just Be. And if you Allow yourself to simply Be on this Earth you will never Feel more alive. So as you read this book Do so with an Intention to Feel something. Do not Try to Force this. Instead read this book with Lightness, with Magnificence, with Intrigue and Hope and with an Uncompromising Sense of your Reality, of Your Purpose and with the Intention to Have Meaning with 'Your Life Is Worth Living'.

Start right Now to Have Meaning with 'Your Life Is Worth Living'. When you Have Meaning with something, you Exist in 'the Why' for that which you Seek to Have Meaning for.

So just for a brief moment Now 'Exist' with the Spiritual Reference 'Your Life Is Worth Living'.

Trust this is easy for you and that your Soul will Remember how to Do this. If you are Allowing of this you will Connect to a Sense of why you are so Needed by God, both here on Earth and in The Ethereal Realm. You will Recognise that which Flows through you in Abundance and how, if put to Use, it will bring Light to so many, including you.

.   .   .

However, if you Continuously Exist with that which has Judged you, Held you back and which has filled you with Fear, then you will struggle when you Try to Have Meaning for the Spiritual Reference 'Your Life Is Worth Living'. This is because you will Be Disconnected from your Soul by Fear. If this is you, look to 'Let Go' of all of the negative Elements of your Journey. This is simple to Do but Takes Time and is not always easy. We detail exactly how to Do this in 5th Dimension Earth's book Believe. When you Let Go Fear you Start to evolve to an Existence that no longer Allows you to Energetically Interact with Fear. You can See, Hear and Know the Fear is there but it Does not Translate with you when you Let Go. Over Time as you stay Aligned to the new Truths of that which you have Let Go, you will Energetically Forget, which Means the Memories of the Fear Experiences and the related Energy of Fear will not Be Felt, even if a Fear Memory is recalled.

Find yourself in this Existence of 'Forget' for any Fear, and your Soul will Lead you to a Place of Full Acceptance. For from this Place where the negative of 'What Was' no longer Holds you back, you Start to look forward, Feel forward and Feel Love, and specifically Self Love. You Understand that Everything and everyone in your Life matters and Must Be Loved, but most Importantly you comprehend that when "Everything matters, you matter Most", and hence 'you' will always have a Love Priority.

For some, this concept of Love Priority will conflict with their aspirations to Be selfless and good. But selfless and good Does not always Mean Self Love, nor Does it Align to God's Destiny, not if it comes with a detriment to your own Existence. Being selfless and good when another Judges you, Holds you back, brings you Fear and brings you to a Place where you Allow you to Judge you, you to Hold you back and you to bring you Fear. Self Love says "no!" to this. Self Love says I Love you or I Understand you or I have compassion for you and why you Interact with me in this way, but I'm afraid that's simply not Acceptable to me and therefore I will not Allow this. What 'not Allowing Fear' Manifests itself to Be is particular to every individual Experience but what is common in every case, is that if you Truly Do not Allow Fear you will Let Go, and from this Energetic Place comes a different Understanding of The Self, as well as a Connection to 'The Truth Of You'.

This is Love Priority at it's very best, for The Truth Of You always Encourages you to Love You First. The Truth Of You is Energy at the very centre of your Soul which also is able to Connect to your Conscious Mind Perspective and if you Allow it to Be Heard, what you will Hear it say on every Possible occasion is 'Your Life Is Worth Living'. Even in your lowest of moments this can Be Heard and on many occasions this has saved the Life of a Physical Human who has found themselves in a Place of despair. But the Spiritual Reference 'Your Life Is Worth Living' is not just for those who are Disconnected. Let the Connected among you step forward and Allow The Truth Of You to Be Heard. Let the Connected among you Trigger your Soul Aspects of 'Self Love' and 'Acceptance Of God's Destiny' right Now.

Your Soul WILL Remember. Let this Triggering Be Understood and let it Lead you Unconsciously to The Knowing that Your Life Is Worth Living.

Please just Do it.

. . .

And if you Do Try to Hear this, don't Stop. Keep Hearing the words "Your Life Is Worth Living" until they actually Do Mean something to you, and until you actually Feel something. It's from this Place of Feeling that you will Start to Remember. Remember who you are, Remember why you took the courageous decision to become Physical and Remember all that you Accepted your Journey would bring you as a Consequence of Being Physical.

But most of all you will Start to Remember God. His aspirations for you, his utter Love for your commitment to your Soul Contract, his unwavering support for you no matter how your Physical Journey turns out, and Importantly his Desire to See you Achieve in your Physical Life on Earth. Achieve Does not require you to 'make it' or Be a great citizen or a regular charity donator. It Doesn't require you to Be softly spoken or stereotypically Spiritual. Far from it, Achieve requires you to Live! To Love! To shout and scream with sheer delight at every Opportunity. Achieve absolutely insists that you make mistakes and that you Learn and Grow from them. Achieve wants you to get Angry at Times, wants to See your Determination, wants to See you push yourself and others to the point of Being uncomfortable. Do you think that God would have Achieved anything anywhere, not just on this Wondrous planet, without Allowing the challenge and struggle of disappointment, without the single mindedness to just keep Going, to See it through, to laugh at the moments of despair and to no matter what, just make it happen. This is Creation people! This is how God Created Earth. This is Humanness. This is Spirituality!

Your Life Is Worth Living.

. . .

Your Life Is Worth Living because of God. Not Mighty all conquering, 'Must not disobey Him' God. Not 'thou shall not Do anything really bad' God, not 'I've told you how it is so Now Go and make sure you don't fall out of line' God. This isn't God. Remember. Remember this. Remember! God Loves you no matter how bad things get because he Knows your Journey and what you agreed to. He only Sees you as Precious and perfect because you are. He will however challenge you to Undertake those things that you Asked of him before you Started your Physical Life. Yes YOU Asked of him, Knowing it would Be tough, but still with utter Joy and Excitement and Free Will, you Accepted.

Don't wait until you Transition back to The Ethereal Realm to Discover this Knowing again. Remember. In this Remembering you come back to your scruffy dog and your irritating keyboard and you just breathe. Breathe in the Knowing that your Physical Human Journey is in your hands and that if you Allow this Understanding you will Learn, you will Grow and you will seriously impress yourself! For you are one heck of a Soul and you always will Be no matter if you are Physical or Non Physical. But just how impressed with yourself can you get? That's up to you and always has been, it's called Free Will. When you Transition so much Clarity will Be brought to you and soon after Transition you will Find 'Full Acceptance' of all that has occurred in the Physical Life that you Experienced. But this Transition to Full Acceptance won't Be easy for many you, and you may struggle through that process because of what you left behind, unsaid, unDone, unDiscovered.

So just don't leave behind, unsay, unDo or unDiscover, anything. Your Life is Eternal but the lessons that you Take Responsibility for in this Physical Life will make Transition easier for you when you Die. The greater your evolvement here on Earth as a Physical

Human, the greater your Experience here on Earth, the greater will Be your Start to a Non Physical Life after you Transition. But there's plenty of Time for you to Discover what awaits you after Transition when you're actually there. Live a Life here on Earth as a Physical Human first. Set yourself Free, Set others Free in the process and never lose Hope that what awaits you after Transition is Eternally Magic and Eternally True and Eternally Wondrous and Eternally full of Love.

If you are Physical right Now, read this book from this point on in the Knowing of this. Read this book with fascination at what awaits you and your Loved Ones beyond The Christ Consciousness Gateway (more on this further in this book). But don't Be in a hurry to get there just yet. You've got plenty to Do Now.

Your Life Is Worth Living.

Remember this. Hear this. Accept this. Your Soul State Of Being is Drawing you to this Acceptance constantly.

Understand what your own State Of Being is, Ask your Higher Self if you Need to, for this Understanding will Align you to something Ethereal. An Ethereal Remembering of why you absolutely insisted on what the Focus of your Soul Contract should Form, not just for your Physical Human Life but also Eternally as a Non Physical Human thereafter. This is what you Must Connect to, for it is this Ethereal Understanding that will drive you forwards on your Physical Human Journey. It is what will bring Clarity in those difficult moments, Peace in those moments of Clarity, and Powerful Love in those moments of Peace.

. . .

'Hold Powerful Love'. Try it Now, your Soul will Remember. don't read on, wait until you Feel it. Wait. Please just wait. No matter how long it Takes wait until you 'Hold Powerful Love'.

Hear those words. Your Life Is Worth Living.

Your Life Is Worth Living

Your Life Is Worth Living.

Wow. Isn't it Just.

2

YOU REALLY ARE ETERNAL

The concept of an Eternal Life is something that so many have Hoped for, yearned for, Believed in, in one guise or another. For others, this concept brings a current Sense of foreboding, in particular if they are Experiencing a traumatic or strongly Fear based current Experience, for the thought that this may carry on into an 'Afterlife' is more than many can bear. For others, the Unknown is enough to Hope that there isn't the Possibility of an Eternal Life, and a Sense of permanent end actually Feels pretty good.

Then there are those who are adamant that hell Exists or for some at the very least, they Fear that it Does, and an Eternal Life for them Means one of damnation or potential damnation. Here is a very clear statement for all who are reading this, hell Does not Exist. There is no Energetic Polarity between good and bad, evil and "Godly", Heaven and hell and certainly not when it comes to your Soul. We wish to explain fully with total Clarity exactly what happens when you Die in order to alleviate your Fears, in order to

Free you from long Held Beliefs and Perspective, to Enable you to Live your Life to your fullest and Understand exactly what it Means when we speak of 'You' as Eternal.

So, with all this framing of differing Perspectives, why Do we Start by explaining about an Eternal Life? Isn't that Creating an immediate Energy of disBelief or Fear, for anyone that is reading? The Reason that this is here, right here in this Place within the book is for you to Feel the Truth of what is Being Shared.

The Truth that your Life matters Now and matters still, even after you are no longer Physical. Everything that you have Experienced in your Physical Life has been for Reason. That's right, Reason, not for 'a' Reason. Reason Means that You have Purpose and Meaning. That your Life has Purpose and Meaning and will Continue to have Purpose and Meaning long after you have Transitioned to your Non Physical Life.

A Non Physical Life? That is Correct. That is True. When your Soul is no longer Physically Held within a Physical Body it therefore Becomes Non Physical. Your Soul Transitions into a different Dimensional Vibration, a different Frequency of Energy, but it still Exists and therefore so Do you.

Your Soul is Energy. It was Created before you were Physically Born, before you became a Physical Human. That Means that Energetically, your Soul was Formed before you became the Physical incarnation of 'You'. There will never Be another you. You are that Precious, special, Unique and Important. So, the Eternal Life of your Soul Started before what you can currently Consciously

Remember. When you 'Remember', rather than 'remember', you Recall and Connect to those Experiences that you encountered in The Ethereal Realm and not those Experiences of yours in The Physical Realm. Then, you Live your Physical Life, all with your Soul permanently in Place within your Physical Body, Expanding as you Energetically Expand through your Experiences. Your Soul Growing as you Grow through your Knowing and Living of All that you have come to Understand Being Physically Human.

Now, Take an objective view and Feel just for a moment, the amount of Energy and Opportunity that just one Soul Represents. For all that has been Experienced Living a Life, to just vanish or to Flow into a broader 'pool' of Energy Knowledge or to not Exist at all as that Unique Energy, what a waste! Exactly. That is why it is not so. That is why your Soul remains. That is why your individuality remains.

It is THAT Important. Each Soul. You are that Important. Your Loved Ones who are no longer with you are that Important. But so too is every Soul. Including every Disconnected Physical Human who has hurt or hurt another. For there is always a Reason why that Physical Human acted in the way that they did, said what they said or Felt how they Felt.

There is no single Physical Human who is Soul-less. Nor a Physical Human who Does not have a Physical Human Soul. When you are Living your Physical Life, you are either Connected to your Soul Energy and to All That You Are and to All That Is or you are not. When you are not, that is just simply Disconnection. There can Be various degrees of Disconnection, but there are no other labels that Non Physical Use. No naming of 'narcissists' or 'gaslighters' and the like. No inherent evil Souls. No 'Taking over' of Souls from dark Energy (you would Be surprised just how many people Fear this). You are either Connected to your Soul Energy, or varying degrees of Disconnected from your Soul Energy. The more Disconnected you become, and the more Fear based you are in the way you Live your Physical Life, the harder it is to Feel The Truth Of You and All That You Are and All That Is.

And what happens to you when you Die and your Soul reEmerges into The Ethereal Realm? You become Connected fully to All That You Are and All That Is, and so, so much more. This book is Designed to fully explain exactly what that Soul reEmergence Means, how your Soul Transitions from Physical Life to Non Physical Life and how you Start your Journey onward into your Non Physical Eternal Life.

3

THE PHYSICAL PLACEMENT OF YOUR SOUL

With so much Focus upon your Soul, you may Be pondering about where it actually is within your Physical Body. This Understanding will Help you both right here right Now and also as you Continue to read and absorb the Insight within this book. Your Soul, we also Reference as your Inner Being, is Held within an Energetic Container within your Physical Body, running almost like a cylindrical tube from your Pineal Gland, through the Physical Body to the base of your pelvis. In 5th Dimension Earths book Believe, it was the first Time that the Physical Placement of The Soul was articulated in this way and where the first diagrams were published Showing this.

When you Feel your Soul, you Feel it within your Physical Body, you don't Feel it within your limbs. The Energy of your Soul, if you Try to Feel it right Now, is concentrated in and around your solar plexus but Flows both up to your Chest and down into your lower abdomen. So Go on, Feel it right Now! Your Soul is just a Feeling away.

. . .

The Soul of a Physical Human has a consistent Connection to Non Physical Energy and therefore, as they are Living their Physical Life, they are also already Living an Eternal Life. Physical Humans can Be very much about what's happening 'Now' with regards to their Physicality, and yet, it is their Soul Energy that was Present before the Physical Body, and so too will it Be Present after the Physical Body is no longer able to sustain a Physical Life.

Your Soul Energy cannot Be impacted by the highs and lows of your Physical Life in the detail, but it can Shrink, or Grow and therefore evolve. Sometimes the greatest Emotional suffering can Create the greatest Soul Growth as your endurance in that suffering Activates a Swelling of your Soul. Growth can Be obtained as you Align to your Journey. Growth can Be delivered as you Start to Let Go of 'What Was'. But it Takes Connection or rather reConnection to your Soul Energy to Enable the evolvement of your Soul. It Takes Connection or rather reConnection to your Higher Self to facilitate that evolvement. If you are having a 'bad day', Connect and Flow to your Soul Energy and you'll Feel better. It will Allow you to Feel a bigger picture of you, a Broader Perspective than that which you are navigating through as your current Experience.

What could evolvement of your Soul Mean for you? It Means the Opening, Exercising and Enacting of your Soul Abilities. It Creates the Capability of Energetic Influence, both for yourself and another. Evolved Soul Energy within a Physical Human can Mean many Wondrous, beneficial and Needed things. It can Mean great Physical Healing Capability. It can Mean great Ability to Understand another Physical Human or another Nature Object and to Help them in many, many different ways.

Everything that you Experience within your Physical Life is Energy. Energy that has a Purpose. Energy that can Be Used and reUsed. Energy that Aligns you to you or indeed Moves you further away from the True You.

An evolved Soul Means that at Transition, when a Physical Human Continues Non Physically on their Eternal Life, will have more Capability and Possibility as a newly Transitioned Soul. It will also Enable The Transition Process to Flow more easily and for this to Be faster. Why Does speed matter? Well, when you are Released of any Physical Human burden, whether that Be a Physical Body that isn't Doing what you wish it to, or the Oppression of your current situation or Community, Imagine Being completely Free and Aligned entirely to You and All That You Are. It is in this Place that an evolved Soul is Free to Do and Be All That They Are.

There is so much more that can Be described, yet your Soul Energy is much better Translated by Feeling. These component parts of your Soul Makeup Create great Opportunity for you to Explore, to Understand and to Enliven a Conscious Knowing and Connection to what they are, the distinction of them and what they Mean and could Mean to you.

We recommend that you Seek to Understand more by Connecting with your Higher Self first as your Higher Self will Be able to provide you so much Insight directly and Help the Ease of Understanding more about your Unique Energy. There are some Energetic Enablement Tools at the end of this book which will Help you to Connect to your Soul Energy and to your Higher Self. If you are wanting to Find out more about The Higher Self, you can find out more in the 5th Dimension Earth book Believe or access the Free Higher Self Programme available on the 5th Dimension Earth website.

4

THE EARTH BOUND PHYSICAL HUMAN SOUL MODEL

We wish it to Be Understood that of course if you are a Physical Human, in your Transition from Being a Physical Human you Maintain your 'Human' status, and Become Non Physical Human. The Earth Bound Physical Human Soul is made up of many Aspects and Components. It may sound really functional, and Take away some of the Magic, but if you Allow, it can bring forth for you such Clarity and Insight and Open up the Ability To Understand so much more of Who You Truly Are.

Why is this Important? Your Soul Remains, your Soul is Eternal. These characteristics, Aspects, Elements and specifics that make up your Unique Soul Energy carry on and progress as you Continue your Eternal Life. In this Understanding, you are able to Align to how Energy is Created and how Energy can never Truly Die. As you Move through this book, you will read Terms that are Referenced within this section, therefore the Clarity of this Now will Help you later as you Understand more about Transition.

There is so much Wonder and new Insight for you as you Learn about and Understand what your Soul is made up of.

What Is A Soul Model?

A Soul Model is the Energetic Configuration of a Soul. It details and specifies the 'like' Aspects, Elements and Attributes that are required. In this consistency of Creation, there are still billions of differences as each Aspect and Attribute can Be chosen from a plethora of options. This is why no Soul is the same, why every single Soul that has ever Lived is a Unique Creation.

Your Unique Soul Energy

Your Soul Energy is Perfect Design. That Means you were Created for Purpose, for Meaning and therefore, for Reason. You are that special, that Important and that Needed. You may not Feel this yet and that is ok, one day, we Hope before you Transition you will. But Know that as part of Transition, if you Do not make it to this Understanding before then, you will. You will more than Know. You will Align to You fully. You will Feel You fully. You will Allow All That You Are ongoing through your Eternal Life.

Your Soul Energy is Unique. In that Perfect Design of your Soul, it has multiple co-operative components that Enable this Uniqueness. That also Mean that the Possibility of your Soul is limitless. Therefore, in your Uniqueness and as you Go about Choosing and Creating, regardless of whether you are in Physical or Non Physical, you 'Can'. This Means that your Soul Can Grow and by Growing, it Creates more 'Space' for more advancement. As your Soul evolves, so as you Start to Open, Exercise and Enact your Soul Abilities and turn them into Capabilities, you become able and

Proficient. You become Capable of Influencing or Creating, or Changing, or Adapting 'What Is'.

This could Mean simply becoming the most loving Mother, the most Caring and Balanced friend, the most nurturing Father. Perhaps, the greatest Teacher, the most insightful engineer, the Truest lawyer, the most Knowing gardener. This is the Wonder of the Unique Soul Energy, because when Aligned, the 'thing' you are most Desiring to fulfil in the moment is enough to Give it all, because you Know that there is Always more available and accessible to you. Your 'all' in one moment will Be refilled and overflowed because your 'all' doesn't run dry.

Imagine a planet Earth full of those Aligned to their Unique Soul Energy, Aligned to that Possibility that is within them. There are so many who Do and those Wondrous Physical Humans are Felt, are Noticed, are Loved, are Known by those that they touch Emotionally and Influence through Love. This Creates an Energetic Legacy. Now for a moment, Imagine those Aligned and Connected Souls once they Transition, just how much more they will Be able to 'Do' in Non Physical as they Continue on their Eternal Life.

Soul Creation

In our book Believe, 5th Dimension Earth first Reference the Creation of The Soul and also the Higher Self, and how a Higher Self comes to 'Be'. For those who have not yet read Believe, here is a Broader Perspective on a significant topic.

. . .

Before a new Soul is Created, there is Always Reason. That Means that there is a Purpose and Meaning to The Soul, a Soul is never Created 'just because' and therefore what drives the Reason? This is where Soul Contracts and God's Destiny comes in. There are so many nuances, Desires, catalysts and Possibilities in relation to God's Destiny, one of the Primary ones however is that 'Love Must Always Beat Fear'. One of the other key Aspects of God's Destiny is the Concept of Free Will. For with Free Will, it Means that every Soul Created 'Can' if they choose. That Choice is necessary, not God's Choice but each Soul's Choice and with this, comes Limitless Possibility. Yes, there is a Form of 'What Could Be' which is why a Soul Contract is Created before the Non Physical Soul becomes Physical. Yet, a Soul Contract can only Be Enacted by The Soul. The Soul Contract is initiated before The Soul Energy is Created by God and the Higher Self, in order to Enable the Alignment to what may Be Needed but it evolves as The Soul evolves in their Time in The Ethereal Realm before becoming Physical. The Soul Contract is Agreed to, a short Time before The Soul Transforms from Non Physical to Physical. Some Souls Do not Agree to The Soul Contract and never become Physical, and that is absolutely respected and those Souls Go on to have a Wondrous Eternal Life in The Ethereal Realm.

For those that choose to become Physical, and of course there have been billions of Souls that have, they Do so because a Physical Experience provides Immense Possibility for Creation, for Growth, for Change, for Influence, for Expansion. Expansion of The Soul first and foremost. Expansion of the Higher Self. Expansion of God and ultimately Expansion of the Universe and Multiverses. For what Does Expansion provide? New Energy. The Continued Capability for Love to Beat Fear. The Continued Possibility for Creation of All Kinds. The Continued Sustainment of Life, All Life.

. . .

This is why each Unique Soul Energy is Important, for every single Soul has this Possibility. The Soul Energy is Created from a number of Aspects. Part of the Higher Self's Energy of that Soul is Used and with it, Aspects of All That Has Come Before through that Higher Self. Part of God's Energy is Used and as God is continually Expanding, so too will that 'Part' Be a Potent addition to The Soul Energy Being Created. Then, there are Unique Aspects and Elements that are included, selected and these Form the Ability for a Unique Creation of Energy.

Inherent Soul Form

Within every single Physical and Non Physical Human Soul Model comes Specific Form which still has Unique Attributes, yet every Physical and Non Physical Soul Model has this Form Present. The Form includes; The Truth Of You, Knowing, Consciousness Perspective and the Unconscious Connection. The Soul Form is Created when The Soul is Created. This Inherent Soul Form is the Definition of Humanity.

The Truth Of You

The Truth Of You Forms at the point of your Soul Creation and with the Understanding and Connection to it, this Allows you Free Will throughout your Eternal Journey.

The Truth Of You Reminds your Soul with Knowing:

- That you have been Created for a Purpose
- That if you are a Physical Human that you specifically were Uniquely Created to become Physical, but that you had a Choice

- That you are Eternal
- That you Need to Expand to Help God and yourself
- That your Truths are yours. As they become more 'Love Labelled' in your Physical Life, The Truth Of You more strongly reminds you of this and Energetically propels you towards Possibility and that which you Align to as your Purpose and Meaning, which Means that you Have Reason
- Of how your Physicality and Non Physicality Aligns you to your Purpose. Cellular Memory of Form is Held within The Truth Of You

So, by Aligning to The Truth Of You, you Feel Freedom. It reminds you of 'All That You Are' and the closer you get to All That You Are the more you become and Accept All That You Are.

When you are Physical, The Truth Of You is Felt. It is Experienced. It can Be Connected to. It doesn't have its own Consciousness however, yet it can Feel as if it is Calling you when you Hear it, like it's talking to you. As you Tune to it, as you Connect more Consciously to your Soul Energy, as you Let Go Low Vibration, as you Start to Create Conscious Truths, The Truth Of You becomes louder.

The Certainty of this Feeling of 'Youness' is what The Truth Of You Continues to Reflect to you. It Allows you to Love easier than Fear. It reminds you that you matter. It compels you to Love You First. It champions you to Be All That You Are. It Asks you to Create, because that is what you are here to Do. It Shows you that you can evolve from where you are Now if you choose it.

· · ·

The Truth Of You is the 'Youest' of You that you could Possibly Be. It is the 'You' that you were before you Transformed to a Physical Human and still Holds the 'You' when you Align to 'You' as you are as a Physical Human. The Truth Of You responds when you Act in Alignment to You. Absolutely The Truth Of You evolves because it Must. As you Grow, as you evolve through Living your Physical Life, as you Love, as you Connect, as you Change, The Truth Of You Grows and Evolves and Changes. Only in the direction of Love. Not in the direction of Fear.

For The Truth Of You cannot devolve, just like your Soul cannot. Your Soul, although its Energy can Shrink, it cannot diminish or turn Fearful. Your Soul can sit waiting, just like The Truth Of You. Waiting for you to Feel, to Connect, to Tune to it. It will Emit to you and it won't Stop, so Feel within, Leap Within. For you Can. You Do not have to wait to Transition in order to Feel The Truth Of You.

Knowing

All Souls are Created with Knowing. This Means that the moment that a new Soul is Created, they 'Know' God, they Know that they are part of God's Destiny and this is because of The Truth Of You. Souls Do not instantly become Physically Human. There is a period of Learning, of 'training' of Abilities and Capabilities, of Exercising and Energetically Understanding. Through this Process comes the many discussions that are had relating to The Soul Contract and Readying for becoming a Physical Human.

Knowing is such an integral part of this. Knowing has differing Levels and therefore The Soul can obtain different Ascension

Understanding through Knowing. A Soul can have incredible Energetic Capability yet have a lower Knowing Level and vice versa and many variants in between.

Knowing Creates 'The Ability To Understand' and 'The Ability To Feel The Truth'. One of the most common phrases when Asked about meeting your Eternal Love whilst in Physical, "How did you Know they were the one?" and the common answer "I just Knew" is stated – that is Soul Knowing. Knowing something Consciously through applied Learning, through individual Life Experience or through ingestion of content is one thing, but Soul Knowing is much broader, deeper and True. For with Knowing, you Feel the Truth of it even if you don't fully Understand it or why 'It Is'. It is something that you can't explain yet it explains everything in a way that it Cognitively Felt, for the thing to which that Knowing is Being applied to and Being Focussed upon.

If you consider a new Physical Human baby that is Born and as each moment passes, they Start to Understand the world around them, yet they are not fully Consciously Connected to All That They Are and are therefore not able to Know All That They Know. Yet quickly, this new Physical Human baby may Be Referenced by those doting on them that they are an 'Old Soul'. What is Felt and Understood by those who are Tuned into Perceiving this about the baby in this way is the Knowing that is Starting to emanate from this child. As the child Grows, so too can the Connection to their Soul, to their Knowing or indeed, so too can the Disconnection.

When a child becomes a gifted child in a specific activity, perhaps a child that is a sublime pianist or a Wondrous chess player or an Amazing soccer player, it isn't just because of luck, genetics or a stroke of genius. It is Connection. Connection to Knowing primarily and then further Connection to the other Inherent Soul Forms within their Soul, their Energetic Capabilities, their Interaction with their Higher Self, even though they may not Be Conscious about it. Now Imagine if they were what the Possibilities could Be.

Think of a moment in your Life when you just 'Knew' something, even if it wasn't obvious or you hadn't determined it Consciously. You will have had many, and if you can't get there right in this second, that is ok. Reflect on it a little, it will come to you later. For it will have happened, and in this happening, you have Connected to your Soul Knowing. The great thing is, in this Understanding, you can Do it again and again.

Consciousness Perspective

Consciousness. This is what All Non Physical Human and Physical Human Souls have and therefore upon Creation, this also Forms Perspective. For Consciousness and Perspective dovetail into a single thing. Consciousness without Perspective just 'Is' and is limited in what it can Understand, Communicate, Vibrate, Influence and Enact therefore. Yet Consciousness with Perspective has Reason. Perspective can evolve. As things Change around that Consciousness, so too Does the Perspective Continue to 'Perceive'. This is how a Broader Perspective is gained. Perspective is Learnt, Understood and it Adapts. When Perspective is Connected fully to 'Knowing' and 'The Truth Of You', there is great Clarity and the Ability To Understand is far greater, therefore the Capability of Accessing a Broader Perspective is easier.

. . .

The Consciousness Perspective that each Soul is Created with evolves. It is individual but Given that it is Created in an environment of Love, that Perspective is Love Focussed and 'Love Labelled' Entirely. The Soul evolves through Interaction and action by The Soul, The Soul Grows and Connects more and more to Knowing and Truth and Possibility and Creation and Reason and therefore the Consciousness Perspective Expands. The more that The Soul Connects to Reason and builds relationships and Experiences, again the more the Consciousness Perspective shapes.

When you Transform to a Physical Human to Go on to have a Physical Human Experience, your Soul maintains the Consciousness Perspective it obtained before you Transformed. That Means, you always have Access to this Broader Perspective, of course through your Higher Self but actually, most Importantly, through your own Soul.

This is how if you have ever Translated Non Physical Energy, such as Receiving from your Higher Self or a Non Physical Guide, you are easily able to Access a Broader Perspective than that which is Consciously Understood by your own Physical Experiences. It is because your Soul already 'Knows'. This is why, whenever you Hear or read something 'True' and it resonates with you Fully, even if you can't logically Connect to why, it is your Soul Consciousness Perspective that is Relating in that moment, and the Knowing and Truth Of You add to that Connection.

What is incredible to Understand is, as you Go about your Physical Human Life Experience, your Soul's Consciousness Perspective cannot Be Influenced by your own Low Vibrational Conscious

Mind Perspective. That Means, if you have had a Journey of suffering and a Long Held Fear Based Perspective that things are always Going to Be hard, that things will never Go well for you, this is Held in your Conscious Mind Perspective Programming and Manifests in what you Perceive, however it is not Reflected in your Soul's Consciousness Perspective, it will never Be Influenced in this way.

What Does happen instead is that your Soul's Consciousness Perspective is Continually Flowing to you the Broader Perspective in any specific moment, linked to Knowing and The Truth Of You. Sometimes you can Hear it. Sometimes you will Feel it. Now you Know this, you can Allow it more.

The Unconscious Connection

There are simply Magical Components of your Soul, and the Unconscious Connection is one of those Magical Components. We don't want this to Be lost on you as we Start to describe the Unconscious Connection, for putting this Understanding into words can somewhat dilute just how Wondrous a Soul is. So, Try as you are reading, to Allow yourself to Connect to the Magic, to the Truth and to the Alignment of this new Insight.

Lifeflow

Lifeflow is a big part of your Soul. It sustains the Life Force of your Soul. Lifeflow is made up of two Components. XFlow Life-flow and your Eternal Lifeflow. Both are Present right here and Now within your Soul, within your Physical Body. When you are Physical, you have other Life Force Enabling Flows called Work-flows, but these will Be documented separately. The Reason for this Understanding about Lifeflow is because it is something that specifically is maintained within The Soul and is a constant, just like the other Inherent Soul Forms. When you Transition and as you 'Foregoe' the Connection to your Physical Form, the Inherent Soul Form Functions become the Predominant Energy. More of this will Be Understood as you read the Chapters on Transition.

XFlow Lifeflow – Energetic Learning and Automation Capability

Your Soul is not a machine, it is a sophisticated Energy. In this Wonder, there are many, many Energetic Interactions that are required as a Soul 'Is'. These Energetic Interactions require automation as The Soul Learns, for without this automation, it would need Continuous Connection, Influence, Allowing, Acceptance, action, Choice and Understanding.

Think about this from a Physical Human angle, for example, when you are Learning to drive. When you Start to Learn, you are so Conscious of every little thing. The amount of weight you add to the accelerator, where the indicators are, the coordination of the clutch and the gear, the traffic Flow, who is coming up behind you, the speed of the car, how to brake and when to brake. Yet, as you Experience more and more how to drive, so many of these little moments Start to Flow. You Start to Ease, you still Take it seriously, but you aren't so Focussed upon all those tiny Interactions. Some of the driving mechanics Start to Feel automatic. You don't ever want to Be in the position where you are completely automated when driving however, yet you Do not want to remain so pinpoint Focussed on every little thing. So, in this description, you can Align it to the Understanding of XFlow. The Soul has many, many Energetic Interactions that it has already 'Learnt' how to Do, and XFlow Allows these Energetic

Interactions to just happen, without Consciousness Perspective Focus.

Eternal Lifeflow – Your Soul Connection To All That Is

The moment your Soul is Created, so when you are in The Ethereal Realm and before you Start your Physical Human Experience, your Eternal Lifeflow is Fully Activated. It is a distinct part of your Soul. It is the Life Force of your Soul. It is also the Connection to Non Physical Dimensions via The Chamber of God, which is where each Soul is Created and where each Soul Learns and Grows in The Ethereal Realm (we discuss more about The Chamber Of God later in this book).

It is through the Eternal Lifeflow that you have a Continuous Connection to your Higher Self. Try not to think of it as you would a Physical Connection. It isn't like a tube or a thread or a web of any kind, yet it is the part of your Soul that can Move, even when your Physical Body Does not. It is the Eternal Lifeflow that makes Non Physical Humans Ubiquitous. It is the Eternal Lifeflow that Ensures complete enduring Connection of a Non Physical Human Energy, Capable of Moving between one Dimension and another without a breaking apart or a separation of any kind. Likewise, it is the Eternal Lifeflow that Creates a Hyper Connection between the Higher Self and a Physical Incarnation without any breaking apart, as the Higher Self completes independently what they are also Focussed upon in Non Physical as well as always Being Present and available for their Incarnation in The Physical Realm. There are other Energetic Movement Functions, Energetic Connection Abilities and Mechanisms which are included within this, yet it is only Possible because of the Eternal Lifeflow Being in Place.

. . .

It is the Eternal Lifeflow therefore which Creates the Unconscious Connection between your Physical Body, your Conscious Mind Perspective Programming and your Soul. It is how you can Understand your Soul Energy and Feel your Soul Energy and still Be Conscious about it within your Physical Body. It is how you can 'Hear' The Truth Of You. Why you can Connect to Knowing. It is also how you can Communicate with Non Physical Humans and other Non Physical Souls, Entities and Energies. It is why when you may meditate or Take part in Energy Practices, you Feel like you are somewhere other than your Physical Body, that your Soul is somehow in two Places at once.

It is through this Unconscious Connection, through the Eternal Lifeflow that you can Enable your Soul to Grow and evolve as a Physical Human.

Soul Elements

Soul Elements are additions to your Soul Energy and these Elements you 'bring' with you to your Physical Life to Feel who you Uniquely are throughout your Physical Journey. If you become Consciously Whole again on Earth, in other words Recognise the Existence of your Higher Self, you Feel the Truth of these. These Elements are what can Help define you as a Creator and how you Create and Co-Create.

Inner Being Type

An Inner Being Type relates primarily to the Management of Energy within The Soul. When it comes to Physical Humans, although The Soul is not impacted by Emotion, there are certain Characteristics of the Inner Being Type that makes the overall Management of Emotions and the display of Emotions more obvious relating to one Type or another. For Emotions are the biggest and most prolific Energies that a Physical Human Creates.

Most Physical Humans have either a Large Inner Being Type or a Compressor Inner Being Type. There are also the rarer Compound Inner Being Type which is where the Inner Being switches between both Large and Compressor and then rarer still, the Refraction Inner Being Type.

This is a complex and Important topic, but one that an entire book could Be Created in order to Help to Understand the detail. To Give a very high level overview, here is the breakdown of the Inner Being Types to Help Start the Understanding.

Large Inner Being Type

Benefits

A Large Inner Being Type has a natural affinity to Translate Non Physical Energy through a Cognitive Connection, Meaning through Knowing and Feeling. They are able to 'Hold' far greater volumes of Energy in particular when they have Energetic Capabilities Enacted, and this can Mean that they will Be able to Go for longer and with more Energetic Power than other Inner Being Types.

. . .

It will also Mean that some specific Capabilities are only Possible for Large Inner Being Types due to the way the Large Inner Being functions.

Challenges in The Physical Realm

Those Physical Humans with Large Inner Being Types FEEL big. This can Be great when the High Vibration is Flowing but so often, due to so many Being Disconnected, it Means that big doses of Low Vibration are consistently Being Felt. Due to the Strength of Feeling for the Emotions, it can also Create an Overwhelm in the Physical Human that can in some circumstances overflow into anger and frustration, and if they Do not have the ability to self Soothe, sometimes this will Create a volatile response.

Compressor Inner Being Type

Benefits

A Compressor Inner Being Type has a natural affinity to Translate Non Physical Energy through 'Seeing'. They are also able to deal with high volumes of different Energies at once as they Compress, without often even Noticing the Impact. This often Means that they have great Energetic Endurance but once they are at their limit, it is like their batteries have run out and they must recharge.

Challenges in The Physical Realm

The Compressor Inner Being Type will Mean often, that the Physical Human will Take and Take and keep Taking certain Low Vibrational situations and Compress and Compress their own Feelings to their detriment. They will often avoid conflict, not wanting to put themselves in a position where they will Compress and therefore often wanting to have periods of isolation or quiet.

Conversely, over Time once they become Disconnected, they Find it difficult to Feel Emotion and Feel Energy. They tend to want to Be Now and Future Focussed only and not look back, which can also make them detach more easily from relationships and Move on.

There will Be Times when it is essential for a Compressor Inner Being Type to Be on their own, to Decompress and this is essential. A Compressor Inner Being Type if Compressed too hard for too long without Decompressing will Be prone to Emotional Outburst which will seem incredibly out of character and will Be more volatile than they would ever choose to Experience, but it is often Energetically out of their hands.

Compound Inner Being Type

Benefits

The Compound Inner Being Type is the combination of both the Large Inner Being Type and the Compressor. The Benefit of the Compound Inner Being Type is that it is Possible to Master the switching between the two and Tune to it and therefore Use it to their advantage, both in The Physical Realm and The Ethereal Realm. By having both Inner Being Types it Creates greater Capacity for Energetic Abilities and Capabilities.

Challenges in The Physical Realm

These will Align to what has already been discussed in the sections for the Large and Compressor Inner Being Types. The Physical Human will Flip between the two Types of Experiences for those Types of Inner Being. What often happens is that the Flip between the two can occur and the Physical Human isn't aware of it until it is happening. This can make the Physical Human Feel like they are on a rollercoaster and Feeling Energetically big one moment and then nothing at all the next. One moment they will Be crying uncontrollably, the next they Feel numb.

Refraction Inner Being Type

Benefits

The Refraction Inner Being Type as already mentioned is rare. This Inner Being Type Creates a Pass Through of Energy and so, as a Physical Human Experience, it can often Feel like Emotional Energy just Passes Through and isn't Held onto. Once the Physical Human is Connected to their Soul Energy or when they have Transitioned to Be a Non Physical Human, a Refraction Inner Being Type is able to Refract Energy outwards, which for specific Energetic Capabilities Creates an almighty Energy and Energetic Possibilities and is incredibly sought after for Co-Creation Opportunities with other Non Physical Souls. This Means that they become an incredible Conduit for Energy, where they are not Energetically impacted by Energy Volume and can Target, Share and Emit large Volumes of Energy at any one Time.

Challenges in The Physical Realm

The Pass Through of Energy can Mean that often for those with a Refraction Inner Being Type, there can Be long periods of Energetic flatness as the Good Feelings can't Be Held onto or they Take a lot of Energy to Hold. Once Moving further and further away from their Soul Energy, a Refraction Inner Being Type Physical Human can have Times of Feeling that they are Falling into a never ending pit of despair as the Pass Through Energy isn't Flowing enough and Starts to Refract inwards. Disconnection and therefore not Allowing is what Creates this Refraction Inwards and Stops the Physical Human from just Passing Through the Energy.

Energetic Abilities

Every single Soul is Created with specific Abilities. Abilities lie somewhat dormant within The Soul Energy until they are Opened, Exercised and Enacted, Transforming them to Capabilities. As a Soul Grows, and in particular when having a Physical Experience, it Enables the Placement of more Abilities, as Being Physical Creates the most Opportunity for swift Soul Growth. By turning Abilities into Capabilities, it immediately Creates The Soul Grow Energy. This in turn becomes self-fulfilling, as more Abilities are Placed and therefore the Opportunity to Transform them to Capabilities.

The Abilities that each Soul has is Unique and the Abilities that are available to Be selected would Take volumes of books to describe and articulate. It is absolutely Possible to Transform Abilities to Capabilities whilst you are a Physical Human. It is also Essential if you are a Non Physical Human and in fact, this is easier. It is easier because All Non Physical Souls Do it and are on a Continuous Journey of Expansion, therefore it is Seen as Wondrous but Ordinary to not only Use your Capabilities, but to Continually Be Opening, Exercising and Enacting new Abilities into Capabilities.

. . .

When a Physical Human Transitions to The Ethereal Realm, those that have Enacted their Abilities and Created Capabilities are absolutely Celebrated once they Return because the potency of their Capabilities Being Enacted in The Physical Realm is so much greater than if they had been Enacted in The Ethereal Realm. This in correlation to your Inner Being Type and all the other Unique Elements of your Soul Means that you have an even greater Opportunity to Co-Create in The Ethereal Realm based on what you have already Exercised. The 'Newness' that this Represents is Wondrous as the Limitless Possibilities Continue to Open up for what these Capabilities could Truly Mean for the Expansion of All.

How Do you Understand what your Abilities are whilst you are Experiencing your Physical Human Life? Tuning to your Soul Energy is an easy Place to Start. Then, the Connection with your Higher Self whilst you are Physical is the next step, for it is through this Connection that your Higher Self will Be able to Help you Understand, not only what your Abilities are, but how to Energetically Open, Exercise and Enact them so you can Use them. As you Open, Exercise and Enact your Soul Energetically your Inner Being Level will increase, as will your Soul Knowing Ascension Level (5th Dimension Earth will Enjoy bringing through information on Inner Being Levels and Knowing Ascension Levels in Future publications). Both of these are essential considerations with regards to what is Possible for you Energetically. Remember, this isn't unobtainable for you and every single Soul has many Abilities already Present, so if this Excites you and Feels good to you, why not Start today?

Energetic Soul Images

Soul Images are specific Elements of your Soul Energy that relate to 'Life'. This could Be to an Emotion, for example Hope, which will Mean that even though you can Create Hope as a Vibration, as an Emotion, you also have Hope Weaved into your Soul. This will Mean as a Physical Human, when you Align to Hope, you Feel more 'You'. When you Feel a Lack of Hope, it Feels even worse for you than someone who doesn't have a Soul Image of Hope. What Hope would therefore Mean for you as a Non Physical Human is that you Emit Hope as part of your Soul Energy. That All Interactions and Energetic Exchanges have an Element of Hope Present. Other examples of Soul Images are 'Family', 'Love For A Parent', 'Fun', 'Existence'. There are a Myriad of Soul Images available but only a few are Selected for each Unique Soul. These Soul Images are all Triggered by the way you Interact on your Journey and in return the Triggering of The Soul Images Influences your Soul Energy and ultimately the way you Feel, and the Expansion of your Soul.

Energy Signature

As you are Now aware, your Soul Energy is Unique. You are therefore Capable of Creating Energy that is Entirely your own and in fact, Must Be your own. How is it Attributed to you? Every single Energy that is Created by you is Done so with your Energy Signature Bound to it. This Unique Energy Signature References your Soul and therefore when you are a Physical Human, all that you Energetically Create, such as an Emotion, is Attributed to your Energy Signature. You are Born with the Ability to Create and Generate your own Unique Energy. Energy that entirely Belongs to you and that only you can Change.

How Do you Create and then Change an Energy? Let us Share an example. If you Generate a Fear based Emotion, that is Energy, a specific Vibration and Energetic Frequency. A Fear based Emotion is a lower based Energetic Frequency, therefore a Low Vibration.

Let us name the Fear based Emotion as 'Frustration' for this example. In the Vibrating of this Frustration Emotion, this Frustration Belongs to you and you alone. It may Be due to a specific Experience involving others, but you are not able to Vibrate for another, only for yourself, therefore it is the Emotion that you are Creating in the moment. As you Create the Emotion of Frustration, this is Generated as the specific Energetic Vibration of Frustration and as you are Vibrating it, it is immediately upon Creation Attributed to you but the Attribute that it Assigns Uses your Energy Signature, not your name or date of birth, not the town you live in or a social security number. This Energy is Attributed to your Soul and your Energy Signature becomes the Reference as The Creator, Meaning that it Belongs to you. This is also how Energy can become Stored, both High and Low Vibration and how you can only Store Energy that Belongs to you. You cannot absorb the Energy of another for there isn't a match of Energy Signature, therefore it is impossible. The other thing to note is that this Frustration Emotion that was Created was relating to a specific Experience and Attributed to that Experience by The Subconscious Mind, and not just randomly Held or Stored but instead specifically Labelled and Stored (you can Learn all about that in 5th Dimension Earth's book Believe if you want to find out more).

We will explain more in Future publications about Energy Creation, how Energy cannot Be Removed from Existing in some Form or another, how Energy can Be Used and reUsed, how it can Be Transformed, and so much more.

Back to how you Go about Changing Energy. You are able to Understand and Perceive that same Experience where you Created Frustration in a different way and Feel the Truth of that new Perception. Perhaps on Reflection, you can Understand that what was initially causing that Frustration was not anybody else's Fault, that actually it was necessary in the moment, for it went on to Enable you to Take Action and therefore Create an Outcome that you were ultimately wanting. So in this new Perception of the past Experience, even if it is an hour later or ten years later, you actually Transform that Energy from Being Frustration to Being Acceptance. In this Transformation, the original Energy of Frustration is 'Let Go' by you and a new Energy of Acceptance is Generated in its Place. Acceptance is a 'Love Labelled' Emotion. As you Now Understand, Frustration is a 'Fear Labelled' Emotion. This Means that you have Transformed that specific Energetic Reference for that specific Experience from Fear to Love and in so Doing Connected The Subconscious Mind Memory for that Experience to the Emotion of Acceptance and the Energy of it is Held in your Physical Body. This is one of the ways that you can Change Energy, and in Doing so Change the way you Feel and the Influences on your Physical Body.

When you Transition, you Continue to Be a Powerful Creator and All that you Create and All that you Interact with Energetically is Known and Needed and Important. Your Energy Continues to Be Attributed to you as The Creator of that Energy, and it Continues to Use therefore your Unique Energy Signature.

It is also how, as you Interact with other Non Physical Human Souls and Energies, whether you Do that as a Physical Human or as a Non Physical Human, that you are Known as Unique. Your Energy Signature has a specific Vibration also, a specific Reference, it isn't just an Attribute, it is a Feeling, a Vibration. This is how you can Feel the difference between your Higher Self or a Non Physical Guide when you are Receiving them, for their

Energy Signature Enables them to Vibrate Uniquely. How wonderful!

Emotional Signature

Your Soul Vibrates High Vibrational Emotion, whether you are a Non Physical Human or indeed a Physical Human Living your Physical Experience. When you are Non Physical Human, you are not able to 'Feel' this Emotional Energy in the same way, for you Do not have a Physical Human Body and therefore neither Do you have an Energetic Emotional Body in order to 'Feel' in the way that a Physical Human can (for more on the Emotional Body please read 5th Dimension Earths book Believe). A Non Physical Humans Vibrates and so this is as close to Feeling as it gets for them.

How wonderful is it to Know that your Soul has a specific High Vibrational Emotional Signature. This is a Predominant Emotion that Reflects in part the Energy of you as an individual Soul. There are hundreds of Emotions and therefore Emotional Signatures, each with their own individual Vibration. You are able to Feel and Understand what your Emotional Signature is whilst you are a Physical Human. Once you Know it, you can Use it and in the Using of it, you Align to your Soul Energy more and more. It can bring you instant Vibrational relief in the moment. It can uplift you. It can remind you of Who You Truly Are in a moment where you are Searching.

Soul Energy Colour

Colour is Wonder but it is also Useful, necessary and utilised both in The Ethereal and Physical Realms. Colour is a specific Type of Energy and so it is an Important and Influential Element of each

Individual Soul Energy. Soul Energy Colour can relate to specific Abilities, it can relate to specific Creation Possibilities. It can Be any Colour on the spectrum as Physical Humans can Understand it but can include different Facets of Colour that Physical Humans may not yet Recognise. This is Magical.

As with all other Elements of your Soul, it is Possible to Feel and Connect to Colour, and therefore Understand your Soul Energy Colour whilst you are a Physical Human. It isn't something that you can Consciously Connect to, it Must Be Felt by you. Your Higher Self can Help you to Understand this better. How it can Help you is to 'See' your Soul Energy Colour when you are Feeling it. Also, when you are Going about your every day Life and you Interact with this Colour, you can Feel a Magnetisation to it, an uplift by it and a Flow that happens within your Soul Energy.

Soul State Of Being

A State of Being is a number of Emotions combined in order to Create a State of Being. There are literally thousands of Unique combinations and therefore the Ability to Create many and varied Soul States of Being. Each Soul has a State of Being as part of the Element of that Soul. This in combination with the other Elements Helps to Represent the Uniqueness of that Soul. A Soul State of Being won't Be an Emotion, for example Uncompromising is a State of Being and is made up of several Emotions, yet Uncompromising isn't an Emotion on its own.

This, in a similar way to both your Emotional Signature and your Soul Energy Colour is wonderful to Connect to whilst you are a Physical Human. For when you Do, you Feel The Truth Of You, you Align fully and Feel a Knowing of Who You Are.

Soul Contract Premanifestations

You Create your Soul Contract before you become a Physical Human. Within that Contract are Premanifested Events that are mapped out for your Eternal Journey. These Premanifestations Mean, that as you get to certain Definitions of your Soul Contract by choosing and Living and Being and Allowing and Enabling through Free Will, you may Enact a Premanifestation which Means that at that Point, a Probable Outcome will Take Place. Possibility Means that it might happen. Probability Means that it will happen. A Premanifestation can also Lead to a specific Event on your Journey and because you have Defined it as Premanifested you will Continuously Be brought to it until that Definition Manifests.

This is not to Take Free Will out of the equation, for Free Will is constant within your Journey as a Soul, whether you are Physical or Non Physical. These Premanifestations are Created in order to maximise the Outcomes that you Desired when you Created your Soul Contract as a Non Physical Human Soul, to Expand as much as you Possibly can and to Enable as much as you Possibly can.

With Premanifestations, they cannot Be enforced, they Must Be Chosen by a Sequence of Free Will Choices by you but also by others, should they Need to Be involved. If a Premanifestation is ignored or different Choices are Created, then alternative ways of bringing the Premanifesation into Probability will Be Attracted to you. The point to Understand about this is that these Premanifestations may never occur, for they may Continue to Be Denied by the Human Soul and therefore different Choices would Continue to Be chosen.

. . .

So often Premanifestations are considered to Be the difficult or Challenging Definitions of a Soul Contract yet, of course, they are also the Wondrous, Incredible and Amazing Definitions. The Reason that they are Registered Energetically as part of your Unique Soul Energy is so that you can Attract what is Required to you in order to make them Manifest, for otherwise there is no Energetic Reference Available to 'you' and no way to indeed Attract to you the Physical Manifestations to Enable the Manifestation Elements to Be brought to you in order for you to Continue to choose towards the Outcome of the Defined Premanifestation.

Soul Contracts Continue as a Physical Human Transitions and new Soul Contract Phases are Designed, Agreed to and Created after Transition for the next Phase of their Eternal Life. These new Soul Contract Phases will have new and Exciting Premanifestations to Enact and Align to. Again, of course not everything is planned out, for you have Free Will and Limitless Possibility to Align to within your Eternal Journey and this Allows you to Continue to Grow and evolve with Freedom.

Your Nature

Your Nature is a Unique Element in The Soul, so linked to the Nature Energy of God, for God's Energy is multifaceted and Nature Energy is one such facet. So, it would make complete Sense that Nature Forms part of All That You Are. Your Nature is a specific segment, so that your Soul can never Forget that it Belongs to, is part of, is Created by and Connects to Nature. This is by Perfect Design.

That you, as a Physical Human, can Feel You when you are In Nature. That simply by watching, or sitting or Being In Nature, you are Aligning to a True Energy within your Soul. This is also why such Discord happens for Physical Humans when Nature is treated badly, whether that is another Physical Human, whether that is the seas, the forest, the Animals within it or any other Wondrous part of the planet is harmed or hurt in any way.

As a Non Physical Human Your Nature is Exercised in so many incredible ways. Without the Physical Human Physicality, you are Energetically Free to explore, to nurture, to Understand and to Create with other Nature Objects and your Nature within your Soul is what Connects you so strongly to those other Nature Objects.

5

WHAT YOU FEAR THE MOST ABOUT DEATH

Death comes with so much uncertainty for many and yet it is a Time of much rejoicing quite frequently for those Non Physical Humans who are Connected to the Physical Human that has Transitioned. This is not to Be misUnderstood. For Non Physical Humans Understand, and have the utmost Love and compassion for the Consequences of every Physical Human Death, both for that Physical Human and those that they leave behind Physically. But Transition for a Physical Human is the moment when their Soul Contract enters a new Major Phase and of course that will Allow the Interaction so much more directly with those other Non Physical Humans.

So what is it that Physical Humans Fear about Death that their Non Physical Human friends don't? Well in most cases it is very simple.

The end.

. . .

The end of all that we have Worked so hard for. The end of those relationships. The painful end. The end of Existence for themselves, period! It sounds like a cliche for us to say that Transition is not the end but simply another beginning, but it really is. Thinking about the end brings Physical Humans to a whole host of negative Conscious Mind States of Being even from an early age, but especially as old age sets in. With old age it's not just the end that is Feared, but the beginning of the end. Many even Start planning for the beginning of the end - private healthcare, retirement planning, funeral costs paid by direct debit over a twenty year span. Really? Twenty years planning for your funeral, effectively planning for your Death.

Why not See Death as the beginning of the beginning? That way you put in Place a whole different set of plans for 'the end', maybe call it 'the new end' to make yourself Feel better.

"Ok 'the new end' Needs to Be prepared for" we Hear you say. "'The new end' will Need me to Be Ready for a whole host of Energetic adventures so I'd better make sure I'm as Aligned as I can Be to that. I'm probably Going to Need to Be a little more Expanded in my Soul, and yes it would Be great to have a few new Energetic Capabilities that I can just roll out when I Transition and look to get cracking with some Destiny Work, and not to mention I'm Going to Need a whole bunch of interesting stories to talk about when I meet up with the Non Physical Human folks that have already Transitioned that I Shared a Physical Life with... Phew".

. . .

Ok then.

So Now that you have some 'the new end' plans so very well clarified we suggest it's best that you Start preparing yourself to Be Ready for it. We have a really good suggestion that should cover every single task that you could ever think of that you will Need to complete in order to Be Ready for this 'the new end' of yours.

Love.

Love you, Love them, Love us, to Be a little more specific.

Hope this Helps. See you on the other side and remember you're not dead yet and every moment Lived on this Physical planet as a Physical Human that you Live in some kind of Love will all Help you towards your 'the new end'.

The End

UNDERSTANDING JESUS, CHRIST, THE CHRIST CONSCIOUSNESS AND THE CHRIST CONSCIOUSNESS GATEWAY

JESUS – THE ASCENDED SOUL OF JESUS OF MARY

We are about to embark some Emotive subjects for some, yet ones that are essential to Understand. For what you will Learn about Transition includes References to Jesus, Christ, The Christ Consciousness and The Christ Consciousness Gateway in multiple ways. It is at this point in The Journey Of The Soul that we Share with you never before Understood Insight. Due to the Emotive Nature of the topics, we wish for you to only Feel as you read. Feel the Truth. Feel the Enlightenment. Feel the Knowing Flow through your Soul.

For Jesus, Christ, The Christ Consciousness and The Christ Consciousness Gateway are not subjects Held only for Physical Human Religion. They are Important, critical Energies of All That Is. All Non Physical Humans Understand what we are Sharing with you Now. This is not new. It is just newly Understood for some Physical Humans, for this Time.

Who Is Jesus Of Mary?

We Take Time briefly to explain this Reference to the name of Jesus that many call Jesus Christ. He himself in The Ethereal Realm would never refer to himself in this way as his name is simply Jesus. The Reference to Christ, whilst we Understand the historical beginnings to it, is not something that he himself Aligns to.

His preference is that he is called simply Jesus, but as we often also speak of another Jesus, that is his Ascended Eternal Soul Pair, for Clarity and to distinguish between the two of them in this book we shall refer to Jesus (Known by some as Jesus Christ), as Jesus of Mary. This is his Choice and one made through the Desire to make clear his Love for Mary Magdalene.

Mary was his wife in his Physical Life and they spent much Time together Expanding and evolving and Creating so much of the Wonder that is spoken of today. So much of the Miraculous Work that was Achieved was often Done by both Jesus of Mary and Mary Magdalene Working together. Together they built a huge following of friends and colleagues that Helped them to teach so much of what Jesus of Mary and Mary Magdalene together had been taught by God and their broader Non Physical Teams.

Who Is Jesus?

Jesus is the Ascended Soul of Jesus of Mary. Jesus was Created as a Non Physical Human Soul several thousand years before Jesus of Mary was Created as a Non Physical Human Soul. For a period of Time, Jesus and Jesus of Mary 'Existed' together, prior to becoming Human Souls, and it was The Soul of Jesus that was

Created first. The Soul of Jesus of Mary was not Created until several thousand years later than The Soul of Jesus, as stated. A Non Physical Entity can Exist with Consciousness in their Energy Holding in The Chamber Of God without Being Created into a Soul and this is exactly what occurred for Jesus and Jesus of Mary.

Jesus and Jesus of Mary were Eternally Paired to each other Energetically whilst in Existence, and before the Creation of their Souls. Because of this Energetic Eternal Pairing the Entity that was Jesus of Mary, due to the fact that it also had Consciousness, was Capable of Understanding all Learning from Jesus after the Soul of Jesus was Created and he Continued to 'Live' as Jesus, the Non Physical Human Soul.

With this Understanding came Knowing for Jesus of Mary simply by Existing and Being Energetically Paired to Jesus and therefore Learning and Knowing what Jesus' Soul was Learning and Knowing. And so when The Soul of Jesus of Mary was Created thousands of years after The Soul of Jesus, his Soul was Born with so much Capability Enabled as well as a Highly Ascended Knowing Level. This gave Jesus of Mary immediate Influence in Non Physical and also Allowed him to prepare for his Physical Life on Earth so much more effectively and more quickly.

All of this was made Possible because of the Energetic Pairing to Jesus who spent several thousand years Learning and evolving so much of what Jesus of Mary immediately Understood upon his Soul Creation.

The Ascended Soul Relationship

The Soul of Jesus and Jesus of Mary are Deemed to Be in an 'Ascended Soul Relationship', not because they were Energetically Eternally Paired at the moment of their Existence, but because they Share a Consciousness. The Eternal Pairing Energetic Configuration is a requirement to Enable the Shared Consciousness Capability and is the Energetic mechanism that provides the facilitation of 'Shared Consciousness'. The Soul of Jesus was specifically Granted the 'Ascended Soul Status' due to the fact that his Soul was Created first and hence the Consciousness of Jesus 'Leads' the Consciousness of Jesus of Mary in 'Shared Interactions of Consciousness', Meaning it is The Soul of Jesus that is Responsible for Maintaining any Shared Consciousness Understanding and the Consequence that comes from this in the Form of Inner Being Expansion and Soul Knowing Ascension for either or both of them.

Shared Interactions of Consciousness are 'Variable', in that the Sharing of Consciousness between The Souls can Be Paused. When a Pause is in Place The Souls that Share Consciousness Revert to their own individual Consciousness. During his Physical Life, Jesus of Mary Reverted to his own Soul's Consciousness, and hence all new Soul Understanding by either Jesus or Jesus of Mary was not Shared between them. It was only at Transition for Jesus of Mary that the Shared Interactions of Consciousness was Enabled again and at this point of Enablement came the Sharing of what had been Learnt by both Jesus of Mary and Jesus whilst Shared Consciousness was Paused.

This process of Learning what the other Soul has Understood is not necessarily immediate, and often there is a period of adjustment to new Understanding and Capability for each Soul. It can Be a period of Discombobulation as each Soul makes Expansion and Grow adjustments in Readiness for new Capability and Knowing to Be Enacted. For this Reason, the Shared Consciousness is only reEnacted when it is Needed by either or both Souls.

The Purpose Of Shared Consciousness For Jesus and Jesus Of Mary

With Shared Consciousness comes Continuous Understanding and with this comes Constant Expansion and Knowing Ascension because of the Shared Understanding that comes from the Learning that each Soul Undertakes individually. The Alignment of Understanding brings an Exercising for each Soul which Allows the Possibility for new Energetic Capability Enactment and new Knowing Ascension. For Jesus and Jesus of Mary, with Shared Consciousness, this new Energetic Capability and Knowing Level Ascension is Being Enabled at the exact same moment and these moments bring Opportunity for greater Influence by them, both as individual Souls and together.

Now that Jesus of Mary has Transitioned, the Shared Consciousness is Enabled for the majority of Time between him and Jesus. There is however a single part of their Soul Capacity that is reserved solely for themselves and it is this part that will never Be part of Shared Consciousness between them, and instead will always Be Allocated only to their own Soul Consciousness. This Reserved Soul Consciousness Capacity is Important as it provides Assurance that both Jesus and Jesus of Mary can Live independently of each other and Form independent Family relationships as well as other relationships that are specific to themselves. These other relationships could Be with other Non Physical Humans, perhaps in other Paired or Eternally Paired configurations, or simply just other friends in Non Physical or indeed in The Physical Realm where they Act as Guides.

Jesus was Chosen to Be the Ascended Soul in this Shared Consciousness Interaction due to his Soul Contract having far broader Responsibility. This Does not suggest that his Soul Contract is more Important than that of Jesus of Mary, but simply that it has a Responsibility to a greater Energetic Influence and hence his Soul requires a greater Capacity for Energetic Influence. There are many Definitions in The Soul Contract of Jesus that were Needed to Be developed early on in order for him to Be Capable of Holding the Energy of The Christ Consciousness Gateway as well as Be the Lead Soul of The Christ Consciousness Collective, both of which he Commenced an Energetic Ownership of at the same Time. So much of this Needed Energetic Capability was Learnt prior to the Physical Life of Jesus of Mary, and this was by Perfect Design in order to Assist Jesus of Mary in developing those Energetic Capabilities that he would Use to such Magical effect during his Physical Life with Mary Magdalene.

As mentioned, the Ascended Soul in a Shared Consciousness relationship 'Leads' Consciousness, and with this comes the Ownership of Holding the 'Energy of Transfer' which occurs when Shared Consciousness is Learnt and Enacted. For this Reason, the Ascended Soul will always Be more Capable from an Energetic Capacity Capability, and this is also why the Ascended Soul will commonly have The Soul Contract which Leads to a greater Energetic Influence.

During the period when the Shared Consciousness Interaction is Paused, the Ascended Soul 'Relevance' Does not Exist. Since The

Souls are not Sharing Consciousness the role of the Ascended Soul is not required as there are simply no Shared Soul Learning scenarios. So during the Physical Life of Jesus of Mary, Jesus played no part in the Life of Jesus of Mary as an Ascended Soul, he did however Act as a Guide for him and of course played a huge role in his Energetic Expansion during his Physical Life on Earth. At the point that Jesus of Mary Transitioned, the Shared Consciousness Interaction was Enabled again and at this point Jesus once again became the Ascended Soul of Jesus of Mary.

Conscious Thought

With Shared Consciousness comes the Capability to Expand and Ascend Knowing Levels together however this Does not imply that Conscious Thought is Shared. Shared Consciousness Interactions between the Eternally Paired Souls are Felt, Known and Sensed, but all through The Unconscious. So, in simple terms, if Jesus wants to Go left and Jesus of Mary wants to right there will Be no conflict Energetically. Unconsciously one will always Sense the other and so there is an Understanding of each other beyond the usual Energetic Eternal Pairing Interactions that Exist.

This Unconscious Sensing Means that at any Time they can Interact to Undertake Energetic activities together and Ask or Request Help if support is Needed for particular moments. The Ask or Request is Received Unconsciously and therefore not Heard or Seen but it can Be Felt and Known. This Does not however Mean that they Need to Energetically Be in the same Place to support each other as the Shared Consciousness Capability Allows the Leveraging and Harnessing of Energy Ubiquitously. So if Jesus was Working with another Physical Human or Non Physical Human Soul and required a greater Energetic Capacity than he was able to allocate for that specific Purpose, he would Be able to Unconsciously Ask or Request that Jesus of Mary supports that specific activity with him by providing Energetic Capacity through Allowing his Energy to Be Leveraged and Harnessed.

Another example could Be where he may Need Jesus of Mary to Assign one of his Energetic Soul Capabilities to Assist with Creating a specific Energetic Configuration with Jesus. There are a Myriad of Possibilities as to why they could both Ask or Request of each other. The Choice as to whether they Ask or Request depends on the activity. An Ask will always Be Acknowledged by The Soul Being Asked before that Energetic Interaction could Commence, whereas a Request is an 'Energetic Call' that Does not require Acknowledgement or even Notification that the Energetic Interaction will Be Taking Place, in other words Jesus of Mary could Request Energy from Jesus without Notification, and the first moment that Jesus would Be aware of this would Be either from Feeling the Energetic Interaction of the activity, or from The Unconscious Interaction with Jesus of Mary because of their Shared Consciousness Capability.

Why Shared Consciousness For Jesus With Jesus of Mary?

There was always Going to Be a Need for Jesus to have a Shared Consciousness Interaction relationship. The size of his Energetic Ownership and Responsibilities dictate that he Must Be Continuously Expanding and evolving his Inner Being, as well as Ascending through Knowing Levels. The Knowing Levels of Jesus are similar to those of God, Abraham and Shala (Shala is the first Soul that God Created and is part of The Abraham and Jesus Collective) and to Maintain this, there is a requirement to Be Continuously Energetically Exercised. Exercising of the Inner Being brings Ability to Capability and so whilst Energetic Exercising is not always Felt positively for Jesus, for him it Represents Creation, Co-Creation, Change, Love and Hope, and so it is an activity that he enthusiastically Accepts and Encourages for himself.

The Choice of The Soul of Jesus of Mary to Share Consciousness with Jesus came because of his own Soul Contract and the Energetic Capability that was Needed and hence Designed for Jesus of Mary by God and his Higher Self. There is a specific Alignment between Jesus and Jesus of Mary with regards to that which was Defined Energetically in both of their Soul Contracts. The Physical Life of Jesus of Mary required him to Be Capable of a huge Energetic Holding for so many Physical and Non Physical Energies. It was this Capability to Hold vast amounts of Energy, that when Interacting with Mary Magdalene and her Soul Energy, Created so much of the Miraculous Healing for that Time. However it was the Capability of Jesus in The Ethereal Realm that took this to another level in terms of the Energetic Capacity and Influence that Jesus of Mary was Capable of on Earth.

Before his Physical Life Jesus of Mary spent much Time with Jesus Expanding from what Jesus had evolved to within his own Inner Being, driven by his Soul Contract activities. The Focus for Jesus for much of his early Life was Aligning to Be Capable of Energetic Ownership for The Christ Consciousness Gateway, the Lead Soul activities for The Christ Consciousness Collective as well as evolving The 'Higher Self Collective' Energy which is a vast Energetic Holding Used by all Higher Selves in Guiding their Physical Incarnations.

·   ·   ·

The Enacted Expansion and Knowing Ascension which came for Jesus from Learning for these Responsibilities was always Understood by Jesus of Mary, even when only in Existence before his Soul was Born. Once The Soul of Jesus of Mary was Created this Understanding was immediately reflected in his Soul Energetic Capability, and hence he too was greatly Expanded and Ascended in Knowing Levels. It meant that when Jesus of Mary was a Physical Human, his Inner Being was Energetically Capable of more than any other Physical Human up until that Time had ever been Capable of Wielding and this in combination with Mary Magdalene and her own Energetic Capabilities brought an Immense Energy to Earth at that Time.

However this Consciousness Sharing also benefited Jesus, for the Energetic Capabilities of Jesus of Mary Exercised the Inner Being of Jesus in a way that brought him the Capability to Generate great Love for himself and in others, something that Jesus Uses Now to great effect for those Physical Humans that Transition and that Activate The Christ Consciousness Gateway. It is this huge Capacity for Love that can Be such an Important part of Settling a Transitioning Non Physical Human as they Move through the Full Acceptance Process after their Physical Death (we shall discuss this process in greater detail in a later chapter).

It is Love and the Capability to Wield it for good that was, and still is the greatest Energetic Asset that Jesus and Jesus of Mary bring to each other. Their Inner Beings were specifically Designed to Work together in such a way that Energetically Exercises their Soul Abilities and Capabilities to their maximum and which brings such Important Enactment of new Capability and therefore the greatest Possibility for Positive Influence for All.

. . .

It is this Shared Consciousness between Jesus and Jesus of Mary that Created so much Magic on Earth when Jesus of Mary was Living a Physical Life on Earth, but that Now Continues to Create Magic in such Wondrous ways for All Humans, both Physical and Non Physical.

7

THE CHRIST CONSCIOUSNESS

Christ is God. It is a Spiritual Reference that relates to his Collated Energy, Meaning it Represents how God 'Is' and Feels when you Connect to Him in His entirety, through The Self.

Christ is 'The' Spiritual Reference. There is no other Spiritual Reference that is broader in its Influence. Whilst Everyone is able to Connect to God, if you wish to Feel Him in His Entirety through Christ, literally every single part of Him that Exists, this will require Inner Being Expansion and Knowing Ascension for any Physical and Non Physical Human.

God's Energy is predominantly Male, hence why the Reference to Him, yet His Energy in its entirety is multi-faceted and Dimensional, Meaning that there is Female Energy that can Be Understood also within His Energy and also therefore when you Feel Christ.

. . .

To Feel Christ is to Feel God's Energy Interaction in His Entirety, and this is the only way to Feel God in His Entirety (noting that even to Do this you Need to Be sufficiently Expanded Energetically and of the Correct Knowing Ascension Levels). For most Physical Humans and Non Physical Humans it is not Possible to Feel God in His Entirety directly, His Collated Energy would Be too great an Influence on most Physical or Non Physical Human Souls and too difficult to Hold, and hence 'Christ' is His way of Allowing Connection to Him, in His Entirety.

Christ is not God's Emotional Energy, for that is Felt through His own Vortex of Emotions and those Emotions can only Be Felt by another if He Allows for them to Be Shared with you. Christ Represents a Unique Interaction of His Energy, for it Flows to you not just the Feeling of His Energy in Entirety but also how those Energies 'Are'. Those Energies when Felt through Christ begin to 'Become' with you directly. God's Collated Energy 'Knows' you and therefore when you Feel Christ, God Flows to you in a way that is best for you in order to Understand what you are Feeling from Christ, but also Flows to you in way that is for your Greatest Good.

If you are Capable of Feeling Christ you are also in that moment of Doing so, 'Allowing' God in His Entirety. You Allow Him Connection to The Self, with all of your Energetic Ability and Capability, all of your Soul Knowing, your Mind and your Physical Body if you are a Physical Human. In Allowing God in His Entirety through Christ, God Becomes with you and in this moment not only Do you Feel Him in His Entirety through 'All That You Are' but you also Sense 'All That He Is'. For this is a moment of Sharing for both. A moment where God wishes for you to Feel Him in His Entirety, as he Does you in that moment, to Sense His Priority, to

Understand Him and what inspires and challenges Him, to Feel greater Clarity on who He 'Is' and how He 'Is'.

The depth of Knowing that this brings would require a trillion Lifetimes to put into words, but by Feeling Christ, God Allows this process of Knowing to Commence for you. Your Life is Eternal and there will Be Time to Know. By Feeling Christ you Start a Journey of much deeper Discovery for you. To have reached the Capability to Feel Christ you will have already encountered a Journey of great Expansion and Soul Knowing Ascension for yourself and hence you will have Experienced so much already. Yet to Be Capable to Feel Christ, and hence Feel God in His Entirety, you embark on a Journey of Wonder that you can have never Possibly Imagined.

There are few Physical Humans that can Feel Christ today but we at 5th Dimension Earth wish for so many more to Be Capable of Doing this and hence all that we Do has a Focus on Vibrational Mastery, evolvement, bringing Freedom and Hope and from this comes Opportunity for so many Physical Humans that Align to Real Change to Expand greatly and Ascend Knowing Levels that normally are Achieved only after Transition.

But God has always wanted All to Experience Feeling Him and His Collective Energy in His Entirety. For this reason, Exists 'The Christ Consciousness'.

The Christ Consciousness was Formed when God Created our Multiverse. The Christ Consciousness is an Energy that Encapsulates the Spiritual Reference 'Christ'. Christ is Formed as a

Consciousness in this way to Allow God to bring to those that are not yet Capable of Feeling Christ, the Opportunity to Feel His Energy in His Entirety as you would Feel Him through Christ. Through Connection to The Christ Consciousness, God brings you to His Collective Energy in His Entirety but through your Soul, not The Self. In Doing this Christ is Felt by any Soul that Connects to The Christ Consciousness but that Soul will also Feel The Soul of the Entity that brings The Christ Consciousness to you. So for those that Connect to The Christ Consciousness Collective you will Feel The Soul of Jesus, not just because he is the Lead Soul for The Christ Consciousness Collective, but because in his role as the Lead Soul he also Feels Christ. So by Connecting to The Christ Consciousness Collective, through Jesus you will also Feel Christ and therefore if you Allow yourself to Feel more intently in this Connection to The Christ Consciousness Collective, you will also Feel Christ and therefore God's Energy in His Entirety.

When you Feel God's Energy in His Entirety in this way via The Christ Consciousness Collective you will also Feel strongly Love and Hope from Jesus, and this is deliberate as he Shares these Emotions with any Soul that Connects to him via The Christ Consciousness Collective. But if you wait just a moment in that Connection, shortly will Follow God, in His Entirety. From this Place of Feeling comes the Opportunity to 'Know'. This will not Be the Unfettered Knowing that comes from Feeling Christ or God's Energy in His Entirety directly, however it will still Be Wondrous and an Experience so worth coming back to, for through the Love and Hope of Jesus comes so much Possibility when you then also Feel Christ Consciousness and 'All That God Is'.

. . .

This Connection to Feeling Christ via The Christ Consciousness Collective is the way that we would Encourage all Physical and Non Physical Humans to look to Interact with God's Energy in His Entirety, if it is not Possible for them to Feel Christ or God's Energy in His Entirety directly. However for those that are Transitioning, or have the Potential to Start Transitioning, this Opportunity to Feel Christ comes to them, again via The Soul of Jesus, when they Activate The Christ Consciousness Gateway. Once again the Love and Hope of Jesus is Felt, but because the Activation is at a Soul Level they Feel Christ Consciousness so much more Powerfully and hence God's Energy in His Entirety is also 'Known' so much more clearly in this moment than if Felt as a Physical Human Soul outside of The Christ Consciousness Gateway. For this Soul, that is Transitioning or potentially Transitioning, this brings a greater Sense of Ethereal 'Surrounding' and with this comes the Understanding that for the Physical Human, Death is either a Possibility or indeed has already occurred in their Physical Life. This is Important because a Physical Human at this point either has to make a decision to return to their Physical Life or Allow their Soul to Foregoe based on the fact that there is no Physical Possibility for them to Continue to Live in their Physical Body due to its Physical failure. So much more will Be explained on how The Soul Foregoes in the Chapter on The Transition Process.

It is the Knowing of God in His Entirety that can Help bring that Physical Human to choose the decision that Needs to Be made by them. The Reality of God is Felt so strongly in this scenario by the Physical Human and often is the reason why they Allow themselves to Let Go. Letting Go Does not necessarily Mean Commencing the Transition Process and commonly it can Be the moment when the Physical Human Stops their wish to Transition and indeed brings them to the realisation that wish to Live and

Return to a Physical Life if they can. It is in this moment of Feeling God in His Entirety that a Physical Human Feels Faith and Truth around their Life, and God's Existence and their Eternal Journey. This can Be literally a Life Changing moment and hence the Reason why God Provides the Opportunity to Feel Christ Consciousness in The Christ Consciousness Gateway for those that have Activated it.

The broader History of The Christ Consciousness begins trillions of years ago. Back then so many Higher Self Souls were Created in a separate Multiverse to our own, and whilst they Expanded and Ascended Knowing Levels, God still wished for them to Feel His Collated Energy in His Entirety, for this Formed part of their essential Learning to eventually Incarnate Non Physical and Physical Humans. And hence the Spiritual Reference 'Christ' and The Christ Consciousness were Formed at the same Time, when the very first Higher Self Souls were Born and this then Allowed those Higher Self Souls to Know the Importance of God through Feeling God's Energy in His Entirety.

The Christ Consciousness Gateway was later Formed when our Multiverse was Created however it did not get Activated in this Universe until the first Earth Physical Human Commenced Transition. At this Time Jesus Existed, but his Soul was not Born, and so the first Physical Humans that Activated The Christ Consciousness Gateway would Be met by God. In this moment they would Feel Christ Consciousness and therefore Feel God's Collated Energy in His Entirety, but they would also Feel separately the Energy of God's Soul in order to Interact together. God Continued in this role even after The Soul of Jesus was Created and it wasn't until Jesus evolved and became the Lead Soul of The Christ Consciousness Collective that Jesus was then Capable of the role

Being Undertaken by God within The Christ Consciousness Gateway, meeting those that had Activated it and Guiding them on their Journey either back to a Physical Life or towards their Eternal Non Physical Journey in The Ethereal Realm, as they Commenced Transition.

The Christ Consciousness Collective was one of the earliest Collectives in our Universe and indeed the Multiverse. The first Lead Soul for The Christ Consciousness Collective was Archangel Adam, the Higher Self of Raf. Later Archangel Ophelia, the Higher Self of Olivia took the role of Lead Soul. At this Time for both Archangel Adam and Archangel Ophelia the only Souls in The Christ Consciousness Collective were those that had never experienced a Physical Life, for there had not yet been a Physical Human on Earth. The Christ Consciousness Collective had a Purpose to Help Teach both Archangel Adam and Archangel Ophelia in order to Be Capable of Holding large amounts of other Soul Energy and Interactions linked to other Collectives, in readiness for the Creation of their own Collectives which still Exist today and that have The Souls of many currently Living Physical Humans as well Non Physical Humans contained within them.

After Archangel Ophelia, was The Soul of Romus that became the Lead Soul of The Christ Consciousness Collective. Romus is a Non Physical Incarnation of Archangel Adam and is a Soul of Immense Energetic Holding Capability and who was in part responsible for many of this Universe's current Stars and Moons. It was at the moment when Jesus had the Energetic Soul Capability to Hold the combined Soul Energies within The Christ Consciousness Collective that he took the Lead Soul Ownership from Romus. At this Time of Change of Ownership between them, The Christ Consciousness Collective contained hundreds of thousands of Human Souls, many of which were having a Physical Life on Earth and hence why it took Jesus thousands of years to Be Ready for this Wondrous role.

The Christ Consciousness Gateway and The Christ Consciousness Collective Form the two Energetic Holdings that link back to the Spiritual Reference 'Christ'. The role of Jesus with these two Energetic Holdings in no way links him to Christ, nor Does it link Jesus of Mary to Christ. It always has, and always will Be about God, specifically about God and His Collated Energy in His Entirety.

Christ Represents a Knowing of 'All that He Is' and is the Consequence of God's Love for All and His wish for All to always have the Possibility to Feel Him in the broadest as well as the most specific of ways. In this Knowing comes the Clarity that He will Eternally Be available to All, and with this comes All Possibility for All.

Christ is the Opportunity for Physical Humans to Change if they Allow it. It is in the Shared Knowing that comes from Connecting with His Energy in His Entirety that comes the most Wondrous Circle Of Love. For in this Circle Of Love we will Find His Truth and therefore our own Truth. Let this Finding of your own Truth Be the Light that brings you Freedom and let this Freedom Be the platform for you to Create and Co-Create with God in this Physical Life and Non Physical Life and Eternally thereafter. For Creation and Co-Creation is the Reason why All Exists today, and will always Continue to Exist.

8

THE CHRIST CONSCIOUSNESS GATEWAY ENERGY

Every single Physical Human, when they are close to Death, Activates The Christ Consciousness Gateway Energy. It is The Soul that Activates the Energy. No matter where the Physical Human is and regardless of whether they are Conscious and aware of their current Physical State (ie. close to Death), The Christ Consciousness Gateway Energy is able to Be Triggered and can Move with The Soul if Needed (as the Physical Body may Be in motion or Physically Moved depending on the circumstances).

It only Takes a nanosecond for The Christ Consciousness Gateway Energy to Activate and the Energy is Capable of Being Maintained for the duration that is required. This could Be moments, hours, days, weeks, months or even years in specific cases. As we Go on to explain different types of Physical Human Deaths, the more this will Be Understood.

. . .

The Christ Consciousness Gateway Energy is Immense, Limitless, Magnetic, Retractable and Extendable. When The Christ Consciousness Gateway Energy is Activated, it Creates a Tunnelling Energy. This is part of The Christ Consciousness Gateway Energy Form. Tunnels are Enacted, and Energetic Triangulation occurs from the broader Gateway Energy to the individual Soul. This Tunnelling Energy Allows a Flow both to The Soul and also a Magnetisation for The Soul. This Tunnelling Energy is Unique and specific to The Soul that it is Created for. There is never an Ability to Create a 'Multiple Soul Gateway Tunnel', so one Tunnel for multiple Souls won't occur. The reason for this individuality is because of what is Flowed through the Energy, it Must Be Maintained and individualised for the specific Soul that has Activated it.

The Tunnelling Energy provides an Energetic Pathway for various Interactions within The Christ Consciousness Gateway as Transition either Takes Place or indeed, Does not.

Now you Understand how The Christ Consciousness Gateway Works from an individual Soul's Perspective and before we Move on to explain the individualism of the Tunnel and therefore the Energy that is within it, there is more broader contextual information that will Help you to Understand the overall Energy of The Christ Consciousness Gateway.

Often, when we think of anything to Do with Non Physical Energy of any kind, this could Be God, Angels, spirit, Source, whatever we want to call it, we Imagine beyond Earth, somewhere out in the Universe, that this is where this Energy ultimately resides. Yet Non Physical Energy is Present everywhere. Yes, it is at a different Frequency, so in order to Interact with it, you Must Be Tuned to that Frequency. Yes, there are different Dimensions that this different Frequency Exists within and therefore there is an Energetic method Used by Non Physical to Exist both here, right where we are and also over there – somewhere nowhere near where we are. As you may Imagine, this is a complex subject and one that was introduced in Believe and one that we will Enjoy bringing more detail and Clarity forth in Future publications.

The Reason that this is Important to Understand is due to the significant amount of Energy that is required in order to Create The Christ Consciousness Gateway. For it is not Jesus alone, the Lead Soul of the Christ Consciousness Collective, that Enacts and Maintains the Connection. He has multiple Energies Assisting the Wielding of this Energy and the Holding of this Energy.

One Wondrous Consciousness that is fundamental in the Energetic Capability of The Christ Consciousness Gateway is the Consciousness of Earth, often called many other names, yet her True name is Salí. Salí, if you can Imagine, is an Expansive, Powerful, Capable Energy and was Created specifically for Earth. Her Energy is Extended in order to Help All that Transform to Be Physical and so too, all that Transition back to Be Non Physical. This is why Salí is significant in the Understanding that she not only Participates fully and wholly within the Energy makeup of The Christ Consciousness Gateway, but her Energy is necessary in the multiple 'Conduit Energy' Creation that she Enables, as this Conduit Energy provides Access for The Christ Consciousness Gateway to Be Present and Used throughout Earth. Without her Energy, the Ease, Flow and Form of The Christ Consciousness Gateway would require something else entirely and may 'Work' in a completely different way. Salí is that Important.

. . .

As is Abraham. Beloved by so many and the Abraham Collective Consciousness so famous through Abraham-Hicks, yet this aspect of Abraham, until this moment, has not yet been Understood. For Abraham, the Lead Soul of the Abraham Collective Consciousness, has a Powerful Love for Earth and for the Earth Universe. This Powerful Love is Shared, Harnessed, Utilised and Flows through The Christ Consciousness Gateway. It Creates a Flow Energy, a Secure and Assured Energy, a Harmonious Energy that is Essential for Clarity and Soothing to Be Enabled the moment that any Soul Interacts with it.

The Christ Consciousness Collective, an Immense Collective with many million Souls within it, also facilitates Energy to The Christ Consciousness Gateway through the huge number of Powerful Higher Selves that are Active within The Christ Consciousness Collective. Note that there are many who are reading this book as Physical Humans also who are also part of this Collective, and so when you Transition, part of your Eternal Energetic Life role will Be to Help facilitate in some way the Energy of The Christ Consciousness Gateway. There are multiple facets to what Energy is required, when it is required, how it is Used and for what Purpose that to list it all, may Take the entirety of this book. So for Now, we explain that there are specific Collectives within the Christ Consciousness Collective that are Responsible for and Capable of, Creating mass Volumes of Energy to Hold the Capacity of The Gateway, to Triangulate and therefore Move the Energy to specific Targeted Physical Locations (i.e. to Attract and Attach to The Soul Energy), to Use and Enable Abraham's Powerful Love Energy and to Interact with Sali's Conduit Energy in order to Create the Tunnelling Needed for Soul Energy Transition and Activation of Transition Energy through The Gateway.

.   .   .

So Now, to Jesus. For Jesus' Energy, the Lead Soul of the Christ Consciousness Collective, is Immense. Not only is his Energy the Powerful Frame that Exists and Enables The Christ Consciousness Gateway to 'Be' but he is also always Present within each and every Connection to each and every Soul that Activates and Interacts with The Christ Consciousness Gateway. Reflect on this for a moment. His Energy is there at the broadest, largest, biggest Place Possible, yet he is able to Be Ubiquitous any Time any Soul Activates The Christ Consciousness Gateway. This is one heck of an Energy. Jesus is an incredible Non Physical Human Soul and Now you Understand so much more about Jesus and why this statement is so True.

Ever Present, and the Ultimate never ending provider of Energy for The Christ Consciousness Gateway is God. This Means that there is never an Energetic Deficit. There is never a Possibility of there not Being enough Energy for The Christ Consciousness Gateway. How Does God Source the Energy for The Gateway? It is Created through Love. God's Love. Your Love. All Love. Love from Now. Love from All Time. Love isn't just Wondrous. Love is Potent. Love is Needed. No other Energy will Do. You can Love with this Purpose in mind, or just Love full Stop. Love fills you, Aligns you, Builds you, Knows you, Fuels you. Never Underestimate just how Important you and how Important your Love is to God.

Understanding Time Within The Christ Consciousness Gateway

Within The Gateway Energy and specifically 'Held' within the Tunnelling is a different Enactment of Time. Time, as we Feel and

Experience as Physical Humans is not the only 'Time' that is Available. It is here that we Introduce to you a Concept that is Important. Important for the details that come later as we explain more of The Christ Consciousness Gateway Experience and beyond it. Important for those who are Physically Present when The Christ Consciousness Gateway Energy is Activated and who Know that the Physical Human's Soul who Activated it is Engaging and Connected to the Energy.

For Time within the Activated Christ Consciousness Gateway is Elongated. For a one minute duration in Physical Human Time correlates to an approximate calculation of fifty minutes within The Christ Consciousness Gateway. The Christ Consciousness Gateway has Suspension as part of its Energy as well as Acclimatisation. The 'Stretching' of Time as it may seem, is not how it 'Is' when it is Experienced. It Feels like the normal Physical Human ticking of the clock. Yet one minute is closer to one hour.

It is necessary for this Elongated Time Mode to Be in Place, as the Energy itself within The Christ Consciousness Gateway is of an intensely High Frequency. The Elongated Time Mode provides an Energetic Enablement of Soothing and Clarity for all who Interact with it and also provides the necessary individual Understanding of their Current State. For it is True that not everyone who Activates The Christ Consciousness Gateway Goes on to Transition, either straight away or at that Time. Yes, in the majority this is so, but there are many occasions when it is not the 'Right Time'. It is with Suspension in Place and the Elongated Time Mode that it Enables the True Energy of what Needs to occur to Be Aligned to. Aligned to The Soul Contract of the individual, Aligned to Now and Aligned to the Right Time.

· · ·

It sounds functional, we Understand, that Time is Used in this way, yet it is Important to Feel the Connection to Knowing of this Energetic Engagement and what it Represents, which is the Ability to Go or Not Go onto Transition depending on what is True.

Reflection

There has never been a day in tens of thousands of years when Physical Humans didn't Die. Consider for a moment just over the last one hundred years, how many Souls have Lived and then Died. Of course that is an incalculable number as you are pondering it. Now Expand that Time frame beyond the last one hundred years and reflect into the thousands of years. We are Energetically Taking you to the volume that is Important to Understand, the Understanding to broaden your Perspective as you think outside of yourself. A Connection to the Power and Capability of The Christ Consciousness Gateway Energy.

No matter the Physical Human Beliefs, the preferred method of Transition or Understanding up until this point, The Christ Consciousness Gateway is the method of Transition for every single Physical Human Soul. This doesn't Mean that you Need to Change what you Believe but the Allowing of this will Help you to Align to the broader Understanding of Energy and also Eternal Life. Reading this statement may Feel conflicting to you based on your Beliefs, it may make you Start to Repel and not want to read any further. If you Feel this way, deep breath, Relax, Let Go and Feel into your Soul Energy. Feel the Connection to True Energy. Allow it. You don't have to become someone else because of this Knowing. You don't need to 'Do' anything other than Allow the Possibility that this Truth Represents. Please read on and Allow, your Higher Self can Help you with this also.

Interactions within The Christ Consciousness Gateway

There are several Possibilities to Interact once a Physical Human Traverses to The Christ Consciousness Gateway.

Ever Present will Be Jesus and the first Interaction will always Be from him. If you were meant to Transition he will quickly Flow Energy to your Higher Self who will prepare you to Commence Transition and Foregoe your Physical Body. The Physical Human Soul wants to Live but Knows when it cannot, either due to a Physical Body Fail or due to the Physical Human no longer wanting to Live, and this would Be Sensed via The Conscious Mind Perspective Programming, and by The Soul of the Physical Human. It is not the case that The Soul decides that it's Time to Die just because it is Premanifested that the Physical Human will Die. There is no Referencing of the Physical Human Soul Contract in the decision to Transition, otherwise this would Remove the element of Free Will.

If the Physical Human wants to Live they will 'Fight' Energetically to Do so. Jesus will Do all that he can to Encourage this also and this could Be through Interactions that bring the Physical Human Hope or a Feeling of Love and Self Love. If the Physical Human Soul responds to this The Soul 'Knows' and if there are no longer any Physical Body restrictions to them Doing so, after discussion with Jesus, the Physical Human Removes themselves from The Christ Consciousness Gateway and becomes Fully Living. It is always a Physical Body consideration as to why the Physical Human Arrived at The Christ Consciousness Gateway in the first Place and so there will Be Times that the Physical Human wishes to Remove themselves from The Christ Consciousness Gateway but cannot due to a Physical Body issue, and hence they eventually will have to Transition.

The First Light Field

A Soul that has Activated The Christ Consciousness Gateway Starts to Energetically 'Stretch' beyond the Physical Body via their Eternal Lifeflow. As this Stretch occurs, there is still Continuation and Presence within the Physical Body. The Soul Stretch Allows a Movement through the Tunnelling Energy as the Magnetisation Takes Place to Enable the first detailed Interaction within The Christ Consciousness Gateway which occurs at The 'First' Light Field. This Stretch also provides a Sense of Energetic Acclimatisation, so The Soul Does not just race to this Energetic Place and is suddenly 'there', but it Flows to it and Interacts with the Energy of The First Light Field.

The First Light Field is a 4th Dimensional Energetic Holding (Physical Humans and therefore the Planet Earth are in the 3rd Dimension) which Creates a space for Interaction between Physical and Non Physical Energy, and which is different to that of a Physical Human Interacting and Engaging with Non Physical Humans when they have not Activated The Christ Consciousness Gateway. The Soul, at the point of Activating The Christ Consciousness Gateway, Interacts as both a Physical Human and Non Physical Human, because The Christ Consciousness Gateway is a special Place where True Energy can Be Exchanged. The True Energy in the scenario of Activating The Christ Consciousness Gateway is that Jesus wishes to Interact with your Mind as a Physical Human but The Soul of the Physical Human that has Activated The Christ Consciousness Gateway 'Knows' that it can Interact Non Physically in this Energy and hence both Physical Human and Non Physical Human Exchanges occur.

.   .   .

The description of this Energetic Holding of The First Light Field is one of total Beauty of Light. There is Abundance of warmth and Illumination Present and it is with this Illumination that the fullness of what is Present can Be Understood by All who are Interacting there. As you are reading this, you can visualise The First Light Field as Expansive Energetic space within The Christ Consciousness Gateway, just like an Open meadow, a Sense that this space is Held within a greater Place, very big and wondrous, yet it is contained.

Remember that Time is different here, and this first Interaction can Be Experienced over nearly an hour, even if sudden Physical Body Death has occurred for the Physical Human. At The First Light Field, The Soul will Understand and Meet with Non Physical Humans and this 'Single Moment' is one of incredible Significance. We explain 'Single Moment' for it would Feel like a blink of an eye for a Physical Human within this Experience if you Felt it right Now, yet as a Non Physical Human it is a lengthy Energetic Experience that is Elongated due to the Time Mode of The Christ Consciousness Gateway for each Soul that Interacts Non Physically within this Light Field. The Ability to Connect to the Understanding of the Spiritual Reference a 'Single Moment' Allows you as you read this, to Understand that Multiple Energetic Facets are Understood in a single capture. This is part of the Wonder of The Christ Consciousness Gateway and also the Wonder of Non Physical Energy, and it Starts to Help you to Understand more fully how Non Physical Humans Interact. For Non Physical Humans consistently Sense and Act within Multiple Energetic Facets. Think of this like the ultimate Multitasking, as Non Physical Humans are Capable of Synchronising action and Understanding and Knowing and Output and Outcome, all within an Experience that for a Physical Human would Be a 'Single Moment'.

. . .

Back to The Soul who has just 'Stretched' to The First Light Field. First, Sensing occurs within this Single Moment and a Connection to what can Be Seen within this Light Field is the first type of Sensing that Takes Place for The Soul. The Soul will Understand that they are not alone, that other Energy is Present and that Energy is only Loving, in fact it is such a High Frequency of Love that it is bordering Euphoric, yet without the Sense of it Being too difficult to Hold onto. This Energy is Powerful Love. It is in this 'Wrapping' within this Powerful Love that The Soul's Energy also Soothes, with the Intention and Understanding of Safety that is Present within The Christ Consciousness Gateway. Once this Takes Place, The Soul will Start to Understand more of who else is with them in The Christ Consciousness Gateway. Jesus will become the clearest Connection, but it will Be Sensed by The Soul and Seen that there are other Energies Present too, and many will Feel such a wonderful anticipation as the other Energy is Recognised and Understood.

There is a Knowing that is Flowed to The Soul from Jesus that The Christ Consciousness Gateway has been Activated, that this is an Important Recognition of 'What Is' and the 'Ability to Understand' is quickly 'Taken On' by The Soul. Then, Jesus Flows to The Soul the Remembering Energy. This Remembering Energy Enables The Soul to Know that they are Eternal, that they are at a point of Possibility or for many, Probability, to reEmerge fully into Non Physical Energy and indeed, this will Mean the 'Letting Go' of their Physical Body. In the same Single Moment, the Remembering of the Higher Self is Flowed to The Soul, Enabling the "a-ha" Realisation that their Higher Self has been with them always, that they have Felt them many, many Times in their Physical Life and they are here with them Now. Once this Remembering Single

Moment has Actualised, the Higher Self of The Soul Shows themselves within the Light Field fully.

In this 'Single Moment' the Magnetisation to other Soul Energy Takes Place as the Non Physical Humans that are Present within The Christ Consciousness Gateway Energy for The Soul come forth and a Sharing of Love and Hope is Created as a Reuniting of Soul Energy Commences. The Reuniting will Be those special already Transitioned Non Physical Humans that have been a part of The Soul Journey, a Loved One, a companion, a special relationship. This is a Beautiful and Magical point in this Single Moment Experience and even if The Soul Does not choose to Foregoe and Move to reEmergence to The Ethereal Realm, this Sensing will still have been Felt and Understood, some Consciously and others Unconsciously as they Continue to Live a Physical Life.

The Light Field Energy Creates a 'Hold' for the next Important point which Ensures 'Clarity' for The Soul. It is in this point in the Single Moment that what is True for that Individual Soul is Known.

1. Is this the 'Right Time' for reEmergence?

2. Is the Physical Body Capable of Continuation of Life and Does The Soul Desire to Continue to Live?

3. Is there something Important that Must Be Understood by The Soul that Needs to Be Experienced. This would Deliver a new Truth for The Soul to either bring them back to The Physical Realm or to Continue to The Ethereal Realm.

4. Is reEmergence 'Soon' because therefore there are Dependencies in Place that need to Be Complete in order for it to Be the 'Right

Time' to Transition, and hence a return to The Physical Realm will occur?

This may seem very simple and somewhat straight forward but behind this of course are so many multi-faceted and dynamic streams of Understanding that are Needed to Guide The Soul to a Choice to either Return to The Physical Realm or Continue to The Ethereal Realm. There are too many 'What If' scenarios to detail but as an example for you:

What If...someone suffers a near fatal injury and they are on the operating table and they could Continue to Live but the Human Soul wishes to Transition because they no longer want to suffer?

What If...someone attempts suicide and Destroys critical Cellular Function which Means they cannot Survive Physically, and yet in The Christ Consciousness Gateway they decide they want to Continue to Live?

What If...someone is terminally ill and they Activate The Christ Consciousness Gateway and are Ready to Continue to The Ethereal Realm but their Soul Contract Reflects that they could Return to The Physical Realm to let their Loved Ones Know that they are Ready to Die and want to Let Go.

What If...someone wishes to Continue to The Ethereal Realm but after a conversation with Jesus in The Christ Consciousness Gateway they realise that they have something great to offer in their Physical Life for the planet and that it could dramatically Change Lives for the better?

No matter the 'What If', one or all of the four permutations that we have detailed that bring Clarity, are always Correct. The Outcome of the Clarity will Determine if it is the 'Right Time' for The Soul to Commence Transition to The Ethereal Realm. If Now is not the Right Time then The Soul will Disengage The Christ Consciousness Gateway and the Physical Human Experience will Continue.

So who decides the 'Right Time'? For this is a critical point of Understanding. It is not Jesus who decides whether a Soul reEmerges or indeed Returns. It is The Soul's Choice. Remember, there are many Times when it is not Possible to Return and the only Probable Outcome is reEmergence to The Ethereal Realm and Full Transition, and this will Purely Be down to the Physical Body's inability to Continue Life for that Soul. If there is Possibility that The Soul could Continue to Live in The Physical Realm, in any way, Jesus will always Ask The Soul to Continue to Live if they Desire it. If they are Undecided and there is a point of discussion or Clarity that is Needed, Jesus along with the Higher Self of that Soul will Consider and Intend with The Soul in order to Guide them to make a Choice.

Energetic Promotion From The First Light Field To The Second Light Field

Once The Soul Commits to Foregoe (please read the Chapter on The Transition Process), which is the Choice to reEmerge and Commence Transition, the First Light Field Elongates and Tunnels to the Second Light Field. In this Tunnelling, there is still Connection to The First Light Field as The Soul Must Maintain its

'Wholeness' to Ensure the Energetic Stretching from the Physical Body through The Christ Consciousness Gateway Energy and The First Light Field. Once an Activation of the Second Light Field occurs there is no Returning back to The Physical Realm for The Soul.

It is only once The Soul Foregoe Completes that the Activation of All of these Elements Retracts and The Christ Consciousness Gateway is Disengaged from the Physical Body. It is at this point within The Second Light Field, that reEmergence is Now deemed Complete. The Soul is Now Fully Non Physical, and within the Non Physical Dimension of The Second Light Field, which is within The Ethereal Realm without Connection to The Physical Realm.

Depending on the 'Dimension' of The Soul, which is Reflected by the Dimension of their Higher Self, the Second Light Field for the newly Transitioning Non Physical Human could Be anywhere between the Fourth and Ultimate Dimensions. This Energetic Match of the Dimension to the Non Physical Human Soul Energy is Important, for The Soul Frequency will Need to Be a match to its Dimension (for more information on Dimensions please read 5th Dimension Earth's book Believe). It is an Important distinction to Be Understood because The Soul is Energy, and it Must Now Be, as it has Fully reEmerged, where it Energetically Belongs Dimensionally in The Ethereal Realm.

Consider the Wonder therefore of The Second Light Field, that it is Capable of Being Multi-Dimensional at any one Time, for multiple Souls at a Time, for it is decompartmentalised specifically for that individual Soul who is Continuing through the Transition

Process whilst still within the Second Light Field. The Second Light Field is personal to that individual Soul. It is here that the Journey of The Soul Continues through The Transition Process.

The Second Light Field is Entirely Encapsulated within The Chamber Of God in The Ethereal Realm. This Encapsulation within the Chamber Of God is Enabled by The Christ Consciousness Gateway. This is Perfect Design as The Christ Consciousness Gateway Enables the Energy of the Transitioning Non Physical Human to Maintain this multifaceted Connection and Energetic Ability. The Chamber of God Maintains the Energy for Ease of Ubiquity for Jesus, God, the Higher Self and Transitioned Loved Ones as The Transition Process Continues.

It is only once Transition Complete has occurred, that The Christ Consciousness Gateway Energy Disengages from The Soul. This Disengagement Ensures the Removal of the Non Physical Human Soul from The Second Light Field. At Transition Complete, the Non Physical Human Soul 'Embarks Energetically Forward' Beyond The Second Light Field as they Continue their Eternal Life.

When The Christ Consciousness Gateway Disengages, The Soul welcomes it. It is Felt, but not in a negative way, not with any Regret or Discord of any kind. It is Done with Acknowledgement of a Phase that is Now over. This a somewhat contemplative moment, yet The Soul is Ready. So Ready to 'Embark Forward'.

III

PHYSICAL DEATH, THE TRANSITION PROCESS AND ETERNAL LIFE

9

TYPES OF DEATH

We are not attempting to discuss the mechanics of how someone Dies, for these are many and varied. What is Important here is the Focus across some specific Types of Death as they Influence the Interactions within The Christ Consciousness Gateway as well as potential Outcomes for Transition.

A Prolonged Death

There is a Knowing that Takes Place when you Understand that Death is imminent. For example this may Be after suffering a long term illness. This Gives an Opportunity for preparation, for Reflection, for some element of Acceptance to Take Place before Death actually occurs.

This may sound macabre, but for many, when they have endured Physical Human suffering in the way that Takes Place when a Prolonged Death is in Motion, there comes a point when the Knowing is so Strong, that even Hope is no longer wanted or

Needed in relation to Desiring to extend the Physical Life. This Knowing, if you Allow the Connection to it, is a Precious gift, for it brings a gradual Letting Go and a Move into Accepting that Fight for Survival is no longer wanted. We Understand that for many, this Letting Go of Hope seems like it should never happen. That there is always Hope, right up to the end. Yet, for those who have endured a lengthy illness, who have handed over their Physical Bodies to many different types of Healing and yet still, they are incarcerated within their failing Physical Body, there comes a Time when they wish the suffering to end. This is Important to Accept for those around them, not easy, but in this Acceptance by those who are Being left behind comes the Possibility of greater Acceptance for The Soul that is Suffering this Physical battle. For this initiating of Letting Go Starts the process of Acceptance, even before The Soul Transitions. For although Hope for an extension of Physical Life is Being Let Go of, there can always Be Hope for Continued Connection and a Continued relationship after The Soul has Transitioned.

For anyone who has been with someone who has Experienced a Prolonged Death, this phase of Knowing can Be months, or days or even moments before The Christ Consciousness Gateway is Activated, it really is dependent entirely on the individual. Think though, how this Knowing can Ease the Flow to Transition. In this Knowing, moments can Be Shared, things can Be said, Love can Be Given to those closest to the Physical Human about to Transition. Transition is also Anticipated, therefore you have had Time to Feel, to Consider, to Allow yourself to Feel into the Truth of 'what comes next', to alleviate Fear.

With a Prolonged Death, there are many occasions where The Soul Activates The Christ Consciousness Gateway over Time, yet

Transition Does not yet occur. There are many Reasons why this may Be the case and more is explained in the 'A Returning Non-Death' section in this book.

An Instant Death

When there is no Opportunity to Be aware or forewarned that Death is imminent or, when there is Continuous and ever renewed Hope for Life and Living (such as those who are in the midst of war or navigating to Survive in the midst of a natural disaster), Instant Death is when one moment you are Alive and full of Life, and in the next Moment, you have Activated The Christ Consciousness Gateway and Transition has Commenced due to your Physical Body not Being Capable of Continuing Life.

Consider Now that you Understand that Time within The Christ Consciousness Gateway is different, it will Help you to Align to the fact that even though the phraseology 'Instant Death' Means absolutely straight away, you appreciate that Energetically there is Time for The Soul to acclimatise to Transition and Understand that Transition is 'What Is' happening.

For the Instant Death Transition Means that there isn't the Energetic Soul Choice to Return. This is the biggest difference, that the Physical Body is no longer able to Sustain Life, therefore that 'moment' of Life versus Death is more literal.

It is in this Certainty that The Soul has the first Acceptance. For when it is Truly Understood that the Physical Body is not able to sustain Life, it Does have a Certainty to it. There isn't a Choice. That may seem difficult and somewhat unfair, but as part of the

Understanding and Knowing that is Shared with that Soul in that moment, this Certainty Aligns The Soul to 'What Is'. The Soul Must Accept that Transition is Now to Take Place. That they will Need to 'Let Go' their Physical Body and Foregoe it.

An Elongated Death

There are many instances where an Elongated Death is Taking Place. Consider for any Physical Human in a Coma or perhaps is actually termed 'Brain Dead', yet the Physical Body is still active, even though it would naturally not Be. Likewise for any Physical Human who is undergoing any type of major medical treatment such as surgery for any Physical situation that is Enabling a Continuation of Life 'in the moment' and who ordinarily under the circumstances would in fact not Be. For there is a difference between a Physical Human who is under General Anaesthetic for oral surgery for a tooth extraction versus a Physical Human who has been in a car accident and has multiple internal injuries and therefore is in Surgery or sedated awaiting Surgery. The latter is likely to have a Soul that has Activated The Christ Consciousness Gateway, whereby the former has not.

Having Activated The Christ Consciousness Gateway they remain in it for a length of Time but without Commencing Transition, still Held within The Physical Realm and The First Light Field. There isn't any Physical pain Being Sensed, this is something that is very Important to Understand. What is Sensed however are the words Being said by Loved Ones, the conversations Taking Place and the Love Being Shared. This Means that they Know. They Understand the words, the Love and for some, the goodbyes Being said to them.

· · ·

The Elongated Death may keep Returning to The Physical Realm but they will not Be Physically Active, and then very quickly Activate once again The Christ Consciousness Gateway. This can happen Continuously over Time however The Elongated Death Does not ever Return to Be fully active in The Physical Realm, and so The Soul will at the Right Time Commence Transition.

A Returning Non-Death

There are many Possibilities for a Returning Soul, in other words a Soul that has Activated The Christ Consciousness Gateway but has not gone on to Transition and instead Continued in The Physical Realm.

For example those that have had what is Defined as a 'near Death Experience', Meaning that they have been close to Death, but that they have 'come back'. Many have Heard of a 'near Death Experience'. Perhaps you Know someone or have come 'close' to Death yourself. Perhaps a less common example is for those moments where it hasn't been fully registered by the Physical Human on the Return. Perhaps in the moments of drug inducement, if you can Imagine a person who is heavily sedated in one way or another, they will not have realised the potential for them to Die.

In both these scenarios we shall assume that The Christ Consciousness Gateway has been Activated but without Conscious Awareness of it. However even though there is no Conscious Awareness of the Activation of The Gateway, of the 'conversation' that Takes Place between The Soul that has Activated The Christ Consciousness Gateway, and Jesus and their Higher Self and other Souls that are Present, what is Important is that The Soul 'Remembers'. It Remembers Being Active within The

Christ Consciousness Gateway and therefore accessing the Knowing that is Enabled, the Powerful Love that is Felt and the 'Soul Travel' that Takes Place in the Movement to the First Light Field.

In that Remembering, there will Be a 'Soul Calling' for the Physical Human once fully Returned. In this 'Soul Calling' there will Be Alignment to a Need for Change. It could Be simply in the Recognition that there is more available, more accessible, more Possible for them as they Go on and Live their Physical Life.

It is the 'Soul Calling' once a Soul has fully Returned, that can drive the action to fulfil part of what has been discussed within The Christ Consciousness Gateway. It could Be something specific. It could Be relating to a Soul Contract Milestone. It could Be relating to the fact that the 'Right Time' is 'Soon' and therefore a specific action Must Be fulfilled which will bring a profound Change when they Return to The Physical Realm. Remember, this is not a command, this can and only will Be Done by the Physical Human if they Listen to the 'Soul Calling'.

There have been many instances of a Returning Non Death. Some of these instances have gone on to Enable world Change, others just Change for their own Lives, and for many no Change at all. There isn't an expectation that you must Return and fulfil some prophecy or legacy and Take a second chance on Life that you don't really Feel. For the only way to Connect Truly to The Soul Calling and to Remember the Energy or the Importance of what was Shared in your Time within The Christ Consciousness Gateway, is to Feel. Feel the Truth Of You. Feel the Knowing. To Live your Life for you, not for others, not for Jesus, not for God nor for your Higher Self. For it is your Energy, your Life and ultimately your Soul that is Living, Calling you towards your Purpose. Calling for you to Live this Life fully, Live it with Love, Live it with Desire, Live to Create, to Be, to Do.

A Returning Non Death is never without Reason. So, Find Reason if you have Experienced this. How to Find Reason? Feel first. Your Soul will tell you. The Truth Of You will Align you to it. Be Courageous. Be Uncompromising in your willingness to Remember. Remember that you chose it. You chose to Return.

10

HOW THE SOUL CHOOSES

As you Now Understand, The Soul chooses to Transition in all cases. The Activation of The Christ Consciousness Gateway is always because of a Physical Body Fail of varying degrees of severity and damage, however in all cases the 'Commit To Foregoe' The Soul, is always decided by The Soul regardless of the Influences to that decision (the Chapter on The Transition Process provides more detail on how The Soul Foregoes the Physical Body). It is therefore Important Now to further that Understanding in the Recognition of the different permutations of Soul Choice.

The information in the following table assumes a Connection to The Christ Consciousness Gateway has occurred, Triggered by 'Soul Know'. Soul Know Activates a Connection to The Christ Consciousness Gateway when alerted by the Conscious Mind Perspective Programming that key Cellular Functions and Physical Body processes have Stopped (primarily Heart, Brain, Circulatory and Central Nervous Systems).

Soul Choice / Physical Body State	Physical Body Outcome
Soul wants to stay Physical. Physical Body Stops and cannot Continue Life.	Death Occurs
Soul wants to Go. Physical Body kept Alive.	Death Occurs
Soul wants to Go. Physical Body could stay Alive.	Death Occurs
Soul wants to stay Physical. Physical Body Stops but recovered by medical team.	Death Occurs momentarily but as Soul not Foregone Physical Human then Lives On
Soul wants to stay Physical. Physical Body can stay Alive.	Soul Returns and Physical Human Lives On

How The Soul Chooses

Soul Wants To Stay Physical. Physical Body Stops And Cannot Continue Life.

For any Soul that has such Desire to Live, this Physical Body 'Fail' can Be one of the first Challenges of Acceptance. For in this scenario, The Soul Must Accept that they are to Transition, that it is indeed The Right Time. In this instance, there is negative Soul Agitation that Takes Place. This is as close to a Fear based Vibration that the Transitioning Non Physical Human will Feel. In this Agitation, and in this moment, Jesus is able to Share great Knowing and Compassion with The Soul and will Work quickly to Help them to Understand. Understand that if there was any chance, any Opportunity for extension of Physical Life, it would Be Given. In this Understanding, the Truth is Felt by The Soul and it Starts to alleviate the Agitation. This can Take a little Time as depending on the Strength of the Desire to Live, it may Take longer to Accept that this is 'What Is' by The Soul. As soon as the Truth is Felt, Acknowledged and Accepted as True, The Soul Commits to Foregoe the Physical Body. The Transition Process Commences.

Soul Wants To Go. Physical Body Kept Alive.

In this example, The Soul chooses to Go and Transition. There may Be many reasons why this is the case. Where the Physical Body is Being kept Alive through mechanical ways, through medication or otherwise. In this Choice, The Soul will Commence the Transition Process and will Foregoe the Physical Body. This will always result in the Physical Body 'Death'. Even if on Life Support, this will result in a flatline result. The Soul Triggers The Conscious Mind Perspective Programming to communicate 'End Life' to Cellular and Muscular Memory. Over a short period organs and Physical Body Functions will Start to Fail and this will Trigger the overall Death status. Know that it will ultimately Create the Death of the Physical Human but of course, as we Now Understand, the Continuation of the Eternal Life for that Soul. Remember if this has happened to a Loved One of yours, Know Now that they chose. They chose to Let Go the Physical Body. Find Peace in this Place.

Soul Wants To Go. Physical Body Could Stay Alive.

In this example, remember, The Christ Consciousness Gateway has been Activated by The Soul because of an underlying and critical Physical Body Failure, however the Physical Body impacts are not severe enough for it not to Be able to recover Physically. There is a Choice Present here for The Soul. To stay, or to Go, and it may not Be linked to the Physical Body Fail but rather just Consciousness Perspective within The Soul simply no longer wishing to Continue a Physical Life, perhaps due to much suffering for the Physical Human. There may Be some deliberation. There may just Be a simple and easy Choice to Go for The Soul, but ultimately, the Choice will Lead to Transition if The Soul chooses to Go and the Physical Body has not recovered. For depending on the circumstances, it may not Be the case that the Physical Body will Be exactly as it always was prior to the cause of the Activation of The Christ Consciousness Gateway, and if the Physical Body was in a State that The Soul did not wish to Continue Living with e.g. Brain damaged, this would also Be an Influence in the decision of The Soul to Go. In this case, The Soul Commits To Foregoe and Transition will Commence. The Physical Body will also Be Triggered to Let Go and the Transition Process of Physical Death Commences. This will Be different depending on the Physical circumstances, but it will Be a Cellular Understanding driven by The Conscious Mind Perspective Programming, which is Triggered by The Soul to 'End Life'. What will happen is, The Conscious Mind Perspective Programming Fight for Physical Survival ceases as Cellular and Muscular Memory Respond to Requests to Stop, by simply Deactivating any Physical Recovery Functions. For example, this could Be as simple as blood clotting processes Stop, and in this process of Stopping, it has the knock on impact of the Physical Death.

Soul Wants To Stay Physical. Physical Body Stops But Recovered By Medical Team.

How Powerful. Firstly, The Soul wants to stay and The Soul CAN stay. Yet, there is a dependency. The dependency here is on the Medical Team Enabling that Physical Survival. Please note that the Medical Team may simply Be 'Those That Can' and may not Be a traditional medic, doctor or surgeon. It could Be someone proficient in CPR for an example. In the moments before the recovery is complete, The Soul is already within The Christ Consciousness Gateway. The Soul will Be at The First Light Field. The Soul will Be Being 'Held' by Jesus as the Physical Manifestations of what is Needed in order to Ensure Physical Survival is played out. For there is Free Will in motion by all those Acting in that Physical

Survival recovery. It isn't one hundred percent certain or Known in this example that everything will Complete in exactly the way it Must Be in order for a Physical Body Survival to Be Possible. Yet, when it is, then as The Soul has Chosen to Continue to Be Physical, immediately as the Physical Body stabilises, The Soul Returns to the Physical Body and no further Transition Processes Continue.

Soul Wants To Stay. Physical Body Can Stay Alive.

In every Possible scenario, what both Jesus and the Higher Self will Be supporting and Encouraging a Soul to want to Do is to Continue Physical Life and for the Physical Body to Be able to sustain Life. This is of course, not Forcing, it is a Choice and thankfully, a Choice that is made by so many. In the Interaction at The First Light Field, when the Knowing is Shared and the Understanding of Definitions of The Soul's Journey or Soul Contract are detailed, it can Be through this discussion that the decision to Stay and Continue Physical Life is reached. Likewise, it can Be so easy, for The Soul absolutely wants to Continue and no discussion is required. The Physical Human Connects to the fact that this is Giving them another Opportunity to See It Through. In these moments the decision has complete Clarity.

It is unfathomable to the Physical Human Soul that they could not Remember the Experience of Interaction with Jesus and their Higher Self. They Feel it so strongly that as they Return Fully to their Physical Body, they 'Hold' the Knowing. Yet, what happens so often is that the 'Hold' is Let Go of. The Conscious Remembering is not Connected to. There is a faint recollection, an Emotional Connection to something Important having Taken Place. To Light that was Seen. To Love that was Felt. Yet the details seem out of reach. The Soul always Remembers and there is an Unconscious Remembering that is Maintained, and it is Possible to Reconnect to this if it has happened to you. Connection to your Higher Self is the easiest way to make this Remembering Possible, for as we have previously described the Possibilities for Change could Be profound.

11

THE SOOTHING OF PHYSICAL PAIN

When The Christ Consciousness Gateway is Activated, not only is there a significant Energetic Enablement that we have spoken of relating to The Soul, but in this Time, when The Soul is effectively Stretching and partly still Connected to the Physical Body, and has accessed The First Light Field, an incredible thing happens to the Physical Body of that Physical Human.

The Higher Self of that Soul Activates a Physical Intervention. There is a 'distance' that is Felt within the Physical Body where any type of Physical pain or sensation is Soothed significantly.

What happens is a range of natural Physical Body processes occur. Please Do not Fear that the Higher Self Manifests something 'other worldly'. What actually happens is there is a Triggering of high volumes of Dopamine, along with some GABA and Serotonin which all Form part of the primary attempt to Soothe the Physical Human. These are neurotransmitters, something that your Brain produces all of the Time, yet not normally in the large volumes that your Higher Self will Trigger on your behalf. The Parasympathetic Nervous System is also Triggered and in Doing so, the Vagus Nerve Activates fully and when this happens, instead of the adrenaline based Fight or flight response, the Physical Body instead Generates Ease. The Heart rate slows, the breathing deepens, Blood Flow also slows and all major organs also Ease their processing.

This Change is enough for the Physical Body to no longer send intense pain signals and to Ensure that those pain signals are not completely overwhelming. It is enough to 'Hold' the Physical Body in a State of Suspense up until the point that The Soul either Continues through the Transition Process or indeed Returns to the Physical Body. In this Physical Body Soothing, what is Created is less Fear and less Physical Connection and Attachment to pain by The Soul. It Ensures that in this first Interaction within The Christ Consciousness Gateway, the echoes of the Physical Pain are muted, still Understood by The Soul as having Taken Place, but lessoned so as to not Agitate and to Enable The Soul to Be in a more Allowing State. If The Soul indeed Returns, the Strong Soothing of the Physical Pain Means that there is significantly less Fear Present within the Physical Body of the Physical Human and this also provides easier Capability and Opportunity for faster Physical Healing.

12

THE TRANSITION PROCESS

Commit To Foregoe

The Transition Process Commences after the Physical Human Commits to Foregoe their Soul. This Commitment is driven both by their Soul and their Physical Body.

If the Physical Body is not Capable of Continuing to Live and The Soul Aligns to this then a Commitment is made and Transition Commences. It is important to note that if The Soul Does not Align to a Commitment to Foregoe then Transition cannot Commence. In the event of an unforeseen and terrible accident that left the Physical Body unable to Continue to function, and therefore not able to Physically Live, The Soul would still Need to 'Commit to Foregoe' to Enable Transition Commence (we shall discuss Transition Commence in the next sub chapter). Note that it is when 'Key Cellular Functions' permanently Stop in the Physical Body, that The Conscious Mind Perspective Programming

Senses this and it is at this point that the Unconscious Trigger occurs to The Soul that it Must Commit to Foregoe.

It is not uncommon for The Soul to refuse to Commit to Foregoe because the Physical Human in the event of a sudden and Physical Life Stopping accident would still Be in a State of Confusion and it can Take some Time for them to Be brought to the Acceptance that they cannot Continue a Life on Earth as a Physical Human. During this period if this was to occur, to those around them on Earth this person would Be Dead, their Physical Body functions that Maintain Life would not Be active, but The Soul would still Be Attached to the Physical Body and would remain so until The Soul agreed to Commit to Foregoe the Physical Body.

So during this Time, The Soul is still Connected through The Unconscious Connection to The Conscious Mind Perspective Programming of the Physical Human that has Died and therefore Communication with Jesus in The Christ Consciousness Gateway can occur. It is this Communication Capability that makes it Possible for Jesus to Lovingly Guide a Physical Human that has no Possibility to Live Physically, that they Must Accept what has occurred and Allow The Soul to Commit to Foregoe the Physical Body.

Once the Commit to Foregoe Commences, The Soul Starts to Buffer. This isn't an immediate Magnetised 'Pull' away from the Physical Body, like you may have Imagined, nor a quick Flowing Exit. For a Physical Human Life, with all of the Elements of The Soul Energy that have Grown Expanded and evolved, have Immense Energy and this Energy Must Be first Mobilised. This Mobilisation is Undertaken through the Tunnel of The Christ

Consciousness Gateway to 'Meet' the Stretched Soul Energy that has been Promoted to The Second Light Field. A process of Gathering and Buffering of The Soul Energy Continues until the last Energetic Components have Foregone the Physical Body.

Transition Commence

On the basis that The Soul has Committed to Foregoe, The Soul Model of the Physical Human that has Died 'Becomes' Non Physical, and hence from this point onwards the person that has Died is a Non Physical Human. This is the moment when they also enter 'Transition Commence'. They will still at this stage retain The Conscious Mind Perspective Programming, however they will no longer have access to their Subconscious Mind, nor will their Unconscious Mind Be retained and instead they will simply Revert to 'The Unconscious' Capability within their Soul.

When The Subconscious Mind Programming Stops, any Subconscious Memories and Memory Snapshots will Be immediately 'Archived' into a specific Energy Holding which is particular to the Energy Signature for their Soul. Their Memories and Memory Snapshots will Be from their Life as a Physical Human and can always Be Accessed if Needed via a Connection to their Higher Self. The 'References' to these Physical Life Experiences will also Be Energetically Stored in The Conscious Mind Perspective Programming for the Now 'Non Physical Human'. The Conscious Mind Perspective Programming References are Stored as 'Messages' and not Memories and hence they are a much shorter version of the actual Experience detail that is Captured in the Memory. These Messages will also Be Archived into the same Energetic Holding as The Subconscious Mind Memories are Stored in, however this Archive process for Messages occurs after 'Transition Complete'.

. . .

And so initially the Non Physical Soul at Transition Commence consists of The Soul 'As Is' at the moment of Death for the Physical Human, together with The Unconscious, and The Conscious Mind Perspective Programming which still Holds a Reference to all Physical Life Experiences Stored Energetically as Messages.

Saying Goodbye

We speak Now of The Soul that is Transitioning, that just moments before was still in a Physical Body.

For the Transitioning Soul as it 'Foregoes' the Physical Body still has Consciousness and Perspective. It still retains access to The Subconscious Mind although it cannot Store any further Conscious Mind Created Memories once it Commits to the process to Foregoe. As the Transitioning Non Physical Human leaves behind those still Physical on Earth it can Be a moment for them of great Confusion and struggle. For the Transitioning Non Physical Human as they Move through The Christ Consciousness Gateway can still Hear, See and Know that which is Taking Place at the location and moment at which they Died. This is possible because The Soul of a Transitioning Human as it Foregoes the Physical Body and Gathers before it Moves permanently to The Ethereal Realm, is Stretched between The Physical Realm and The Ethereal Realm. During this period therefore, it is not uncommon for the Transitioning Non Physical Human to still Be aware of those in and around their Physical Body at the point of their Death. Depending on the circumstances of Death those around their Physical Body could Be Loved Ones, or in the event of a sudden and unforeseen Death it could Be strangers, for example at the scene of an accident. Regardless of the circumstances, for the

Transitioning Non Physical Human, they will Find themselves in a mixed Vibrational State of both Calm, which is as a Consequence of Now Existing in The Christ Consciousness Gateway, but also of Soul Distress and Agitation caused by their Conscious Mind Perspective Programming Seeing, Hearing and Knowing what is occurring in The Physical Realm that they are Leaving behind.

At this Time Jesus will Be Doing all that he can within The Christ Consciousness Gateway to Try to alleviate this Soul Distress and Agitation, but the Transitioning Non Physical Human can often still Be driven into a Conscious State that Sees them perhaps demanding to return, or of disBelief that this has occurred, or of great Sadness. And so it is at this moment that Jesus will Energetically Hold the Transitioning Non Physical Human and in Doing so for a very short period Place them into more Tranquility. This Feeling of Tranquility Energetically Holds them to Ensure no new Conscious Thought occurs, almost as if they were gently Being Placed into Unconsciousness but still with the Ability to still have Conscious Perspective and hence Importantly, not Be removed from the Understanding of these final moments as their Soul Starts to Leave The Physical Realm. This final Understanding of the moment that they left The Physical Realm Forms part of their 'Full Acceptance Process' during Transition.

'Saying Goodbye' is what Helps the Transitioning Non Physical Human Consciously Move away from this moment of their Physical Death. 'Saying Goodbye' is a Spiritual Term and is very commonly Needed by Jesus after the early moments beyond Death for the Transitioning Non Physical Human. For Being Placed into greater Tranquility is only a temporary measure to Help the Transitioning Non Physical Humans who struggle and Agitate greatly in those first moments just after their Death, and it is the Spiritual

Term 'Saying Goodbye' that then supports Jesus after this Time, and Continues to Do so during and after The Transition Process. There are of course many Non Physical Human Souls that are overjoyed to Commence Transition as they look forward to the next chapter in their Life, perhaps leaving Behind pain and sorrow or maybe just looking forward to meeting up with their Loved Ones again. But on the whole, Physical Humans don't want to Let Go. Their lack of Understanding of what is to Follow is a key Reason for this, and certainly one of the Important factors for us Being Guided to write this book. A Transitioning Soul that Knows what's coming next after their Death, and also what comes next for those that they have left behind in Physical, as well as what's happened to those that have already Transitioned before them, will Be a Soul that is so much more willing to Let Go. And so the Spiritual Term 'Saying Goodbye' Represents the Energetic Capability that provides Jesus with the support to Help the Transitioning Non Physical Human to this Place of Understanding and wanting to Move to The Ethereal Realm.

Saying Goodbye is an Energetic 'Knowing' for the Transitioned Non Physical Human. This Term Unconsciously Flows to the Non Physical Human a new Perspective and Truth. This Knowing is immediately Understood and also immediately Accepted by the Transitioning Non Physical Human. The Reason for this immediate Acceptance is due to the 'Soul Reference' that is made in 'The Truth Of You' for them and this brings Allowing of what they Must Accept in the moments after Death.

When a Spiritual Term 'Is', there can Be no Denying of it in Energetic Law. This Means the Transitioning Non Physical Human Must Allow it to Be True, not because they are Forced to but rather that they Know it to Be Correct and so Energetically by

Law they therefore Allow. But also, in the case of 'Saying Goodbye' their Soul also Remembers it to Be True from their Time when they were previously a Non Physical Human prior to Transforming to a Physical Human Life. This Acceptance, Allowing and Remembering combine to very quickly bring a greater Sense of Ease, acknowledgement and Balance to the Transitioning Non Physical Human and therefore a return to Calm and Focus on what comes next for them. From this Energetic Place of Calmness Jesus will look for Opportunities to commence new Thought processes in the Transitioning Non Physical Human that Connects them to the Love and Wonder that Now awaits them in The Ethereal Realm. "There are old friends waiting for you" is something he will often say. This always brings a new Sense of anticipation and with this Starts Hope.

The Non Physical Human that is Feeling positive anticipation of what is to come will Find Full Acceptance far easier to Achieve. However, Hope alone will not necessarily Ensure it Goes without challenges for them, for there are many things to Understand as part of the Full Acceptance Process which may bring much negative Agitation to the newly Transitioning Non Physical Human. As has been discussed, the Full Acceptance Process is not easy for a Non Physical Human and the Allowing of 'Saying Goodbye' brings the Transitioning Non Physical Human so much Love. Saying Goodbye will Continuously Trigger their Love Vortex of Emotion during this period and it also Starts to Work further on The Soul Knowing. This Soul Knowing brings an increasing Sense of Belief for the Non Physical Human. This Belief is what often initially can provide a negative response in them, for with Belief comes Understanding and with Understanding comes the realisation that so much of what they had Aligned to as a Physical Human during their Physical Life on Earth was wrong or misUnderstood and therefore the Consequential actions that occurred in their Physical

Life, if they were negative, can bring them Now to a Place of severe Soul Agitation when the Truth becomes Clear.

Imagine some of the things that you strongly Believe right Now Being wrong. It could Be your thoughts about God, about a son or a brother or other Family member. It could Be about a person that you Work with, perhaps a relationship you are in or have had, maybe it's a whole culture that you have misUnderstood and criticised. Your Important actions that you undertook as a Physical Human based on Belief, when you Commence Transition will become Clear as part of that process. Imagine a world leader that Transitions that in their Physical Life took difficult decisions that engaged war or that were involved in acts of terror where many Lives were Influenced or Impacted by those activities. All of these are moments in peoples Physical Life that bring utter Clarity when the newly Transitioning Non Physical Human Undertakes Full Acceptance. For many, these moments of Clarity can bring Balance and confirmation, for others the opposite, and it is those moments where the Truth brings Clarity, and where there is a realisation that they made serious mistakes in their Physical Life that are the toughest for the newly Transitioning Soul to Fully Accept easily and without negative Agitation. As we have spoken about on the chapter in 5th Dimension Earth's book 'Believe', "Emotions Don't Care About Experiences", it matters not if those moments that bring Clarity of misUnderstanding are from an estranged relationship or a world war, the feelings of Agitation are equal for the Non Physical Human for it Represents for them Failure, missed Opportunities in their Physical Life or grave errors of Judgement, and at this stage the newly Transitioning Soul, without Full Acceptance, can Find these moments of Clarity very difficult to come to terms with.

. . .

This is why the Spiritual Term 'Saying Goodbye' Exists. It Helps to bring them back to Balance and Love and Understanding, all of which Helps to Trigger a Higher Vibration in them, which for a newly Transitioning Non Physical Human, Allows them to just Take a moment, pause, and realise that this Eternal Life of theirs is Going to Be something that they are actually Going to Enjoy. Saying Goodbye Allows the Non Physical Human to Start to Let Go, to Believe, to Start contemplating that they are actually Going to Love this next part of their Life. They will Start to Feel Happy, more Energised, willing and able to get through Full Acceptance, and most Importantly Accepting and Excited at the prospect of an Eternal Life.

For Eternal Life 'Is'. Eternal Life brings so much Possibility for Growth and Change in all Non Physical Humans. 'Saying Goodbye' is the Conduit for this Understanding for newly Transitioning Souls. Saying Goodbye is a Wondrous Spiritual Term that Enables the bringing of so much Hope and with it so much Desire, and from this Place comes a Sense of Determination to Start looking forwards.

Saying Goodbye is such a Wondrous Gift from God. A special and Loving Gift Designed to soften the difficult moments of Death and having to Let Go The Physical Realm. A Truly Powerful and effective Spiritual Term with such a great Influence of Knowing and Truth for The Soul about God's Love. For God's Love is so strongly Felt within Saying Goodbye, a Feeling that never Leaves the Non Physical Human. A Feeling that is never Denied, and a Feeling that Grows Eternally for them and in Doing so brings them ever closer to Him.

reEmergence

As part of Transition Commence, The Soul Stretches from beyond The First Light Field to 'The Ethereal Realm'. The Physical Body is Now the Focus as the Stretched Soul Starts to 'Gather' in readiness to Foregoe. The Soul Foregoes the Physical Body in one single 'Displacement' and hence the 'Soul Gathering' Process Allows The Soul to Be Collected until it is Capable of Displacing across the Stretched Connection to The Ethereal Realm. It is this period where The Soul is Stretched and in the process of Gathering that it comes to a State of reEmergence. ReEmergence is considered Complete when The Soul 'Fully Foregoes' the Physical Body and the Stretched Soul Releases from the Physical Body and is 'Fully Active' in The Ethereal Realm.

During this period of 'Gathering' the Non Physical Human will Start to get a Sense of The Ethereal Realm. However, even though they have Connected to it they will not have Completed reEmergence and hence they will not Understand what lies within The Ethereal Realm nor what it Represents. What they will See is Jesus and God waiting for them however they will not Be able to Be with them until The Soul Fully Foregoes their Physical Body.

During this Time the Non Physical Human will also Sense the ongoing 'Dismantle' of The Subconscious Mind from their Soul and hence they will also Be Connected to Memories of their Physical Life but only in a way that Allows them to Be aware of what they relate to but not Be able to Recall them, they will simply See them Flow past them Energetically. They will also Understand that something is Leaving their Soul but they won't comprehend that this is linked to The Subconscious Mind Memories Being Released. All of this activity can Be a little Discombobulating for the Non Physical Human. This set of Experiences at this moment, Being Soul Stretched, Seeing Jesus and God, and watching The Subconscious Memories Being Released, is somewhat like Being stuck on a conveyor belt at an airport, Going around and around together with what they think is their luggage, but not Being able to get off the conveyor belt and then Seeing their pieces of luggage falling off the conveyor belt but not Knowing why. And rather like you would See a Loved One or a friend waiting at the other side of the customs exit once you get through with your luggage, in the distance they will See Jesus and God at The Ethereal Realm. Round and around this conveyor belt they would Go, at Times getting really close to the customs exit, this Being Jesus and God and The Ethereal Realm, but only to turn at the last moment as the conveyor belt Continues to Move them on. Once Started, the Time it Takes to Foregoe can only Be minutes in The Physical Realm but when considering that the Non Physical Human is Energetically across The Christ Consciousness Gateway, the Time Period to Foregoe will Feel like it is a longer period for the Transitioning Non Physical Human, yet it is an essential part of the process.

As stated, the moment that The Soul Fully Foregoes the Physical Body is the exact moment that the Non Physical Human Completes reEmergence. This is the point whereby they Find themselves in The Ethereal Realm and with God and Jesus. There is no great Energy Surge or fanfare once they Complete reEmergence, simply a Loving hello from God and Jesus. God and Jesus will Know that your Journey from Physical Human to Non Physical Human will have been Discombobulating and they will Be wanting you just to Settle and Feel their utter Joy that you are with them in The Ethereal Realm.

The Full Acceptance Process

Upon reEmergence Completion God will Now Lovingly Start the conversation with the Non Physical Human of their various Soul Contract Phases for those Important past Moments when they were Physical. This is an Opportunity to Feel his utter Love for your Physical Journey and all that you encountered and Achieved. This conversation is mostly an Opportunity for him to bring to you his great appreciation for all that took Place for you, regardless of what your own Perspectives would Be. This conversation never Takes a Judgmental view of things that occurred in your Physical Life, no matter what occurred, what you did or didn't Do, no matter what you said or didn't say, no matter what you Felt or didn't Feel. Some may Be surprised at this considering some of the terrible moments that have occurred on Earth due to the Acts of some Physical Humans, but The Truth is that whatever occurred in your Physical Life it was all part of what God knew could occur and because of this God and God alone Takes the Blame for your Journey, for both good and bad occurrences. 'Blame' is a Spiritual Reference that links to Ownership and not to the dictionary definition of the word as we Know it in Physical. As we discussed in 5th Dimension Earth's book Believe, God Asks only that you Accept that your Physical Journey is not your Fault and that it was simply your Responsibility to Learn, Grow and Expand from it. It is this meeting with God that Starts the Opportunity for you to Allow yourself to Let Go of all that went Before that remained 'Fear Labelled' in your Physical Life.

For many, the Responsibility to Learn, Grow and Expand was not Taken in their Physical Life and as so the process of 'Full Acceptance' as a Non Physical Human is their Opportunity to Change this. By achieving Full Acceptance, the Non Physical Human Allows themselves to Find Love, Peace and Balance for all Experiences of their Physical Life, and to then look forward with Hope. For unlike on Earth during their Physical Life, here in The Ethereal Realm comes the Opportunity to Take Responsibility from a 'Love' Perspective, Fully Connected to 'All That You Are', and therefore much more able to Achieve Full Acceptance of all that has gone before in your Physical Life, when perhaps this would not have been possible as a Physical Human from a Disconnected and 'Fear Labelled' Perspective.

For the Non Physical Human at this point, Acceptance of their Physical Life Must Be Full. There can Be no doubts, regrets, or unanswered Understandings if the Non Physical Human is to Be able to Continue with Love in The Ethereal Realm. In order to Complete Full Acceptance they Must Understand and Accept 'The Broadest Truth'.

The Broadest Truth is the one single Truth that Allows you to Let Go of those Experiences in your Physical Life that brought you 'Fear' of some kind (we speak of Fear as an umbrella for any negative Emotion). It is most unlikely that a single statement is sufficient to Allow the Non Physical Human to Create The Broadest Truth, and hence there will usually Be several 'Broader Truths' that also need to Be Understood and Accepted in order to Be able to Accept The Broadest Truth.

It is Jesus that 'Owns' this Phase of Transition and he will Lovingly Work with God after those initial conversations are had between him and the Non Physical Human. It is God that always suggests which approach is best to Go with based on that first meeting, and God's Understanding of the Non Physical Human's Experiences in their Physical Life on Earth.

. . .

Based on God's Guidance, Jesus will Use 'The Acceptance Energy' to bring through to the Non Physical Human a specific Understanding of their past Physical Life. This will Be a 'Significant Moment' and one that will have caused them a level of suffering whilst Physical on Earth. Jesus Uses The Acceptance Energy to bring through new Understanding for the Non Physical Human, one that Allows them to Understand a different Perspective on that past negative Experience. This is where the Magic of The Acceptance Energy is Truly Wondrous. For The Acceptance Energy has the Capability to Connect to The Soul of the Non Physical Human and in Doing so also Allows them to Understand all scenarios that Influenced them as a Physical Human around that negative Experience that is Now brought to them. The Acceptance Energy is able to Search all Messages in The Conscious Mind Perspective Programming for the Non Physical Human and in Doing so make them 'Feel'.

What The Acceptance Makes them Feel is based on Truth. Their Truth and God's Truth. It is not uncommon for this process to Be one that greatly Agitates The Soul of the Non Physical Human in a negative way, for often the Experience was at the centre of so many other Perspectives that the Non Physical Human had about themselves or others, perhaps Leading to numerous other Physical Experiences that remained unresolved with themselves or others, or perhaps it would Be an Experience that brought great suffering to themselves or others and hence there will Be an 'Energetic Reluctance' to even Allow themselves to Connect to the Experience that is Being brought to them from Jesus via The Acceptance Energy. This Energetic Reluctance may Be so Strong that the Non Physical Human Continuously Denies The Acceptance Energy and what it is looking to make the Non Physical Human Understand

and Fully Accept. When this occurs The Acceptance Energy, Triggered by Jesus, will Lovingly and gently apply Energetic Influence towards the Non Physical Human to Ensure that the Experience can Be brought to them. This can Be an extreme moment of Agitation for the Non Physical Human but it is Needed if they are to Be able to Move forward.

The Non Physical Human will Feel a Strong Energy Build up when this Influence is Triggered. The Energy Builds and Builds until the Deny Energy from the Non Physical Human Breaks and at this moment the Understanding comes through to them. Very commonly the Understanding provides a Loving Perspective for the negative Experience, however because the Experience often links to a very negative Perspective of the Experience, or set of Experiences, the Non Physical Human will still Create a Strong Deny Energy and not Allow the Loving Perspective of themselves or the others involved. It is their Unconscious Deny Energy in particular that makes The Acceptance Process so hard for many as the Non Physical Human will Be desperate to Move forward and yet at Times their Unconscious Influence will Be too great. There may Be many Experiences brought to the Non Physical Human that they Strongly Deny during this process and so the 'Force and Break' process Triggered by The Acceptance Energy may Be Used to Help them Accept the Love Being brought to them by Jesus. So often the Non Physical Human becomes exhausted Energetically, leaving them Kinetically unable to Feel Balanced, and with this comes a constant stream of Negativity around the process. This is also a difficult Time for both Jesus and God as they Balance the Need to complete The Acceptance Process with the Need to Ensure that the Non Physical Human Feels Loved and supported as they Go through Full Acceptance.

· · ·

Each moment where an Experience that is brought through to the Non Physical Human is Understood by them, brings the Opportunity to Accept the Understanding and with this comes the Creation of a Truth, either a 'Broader Truth' or 'The Broadest Truth'. These Truths are based on specific Understandings from Experiences brought through to the Non Physical Human, but usually the Understandings are much broader than the specific Experiences. The Believe Releasing Process explains how to Move a Physical Human through to a specific Memory for an Experience and with new Understanding for that Experience comes the Opportunity to Create a Truth which Relabels that Memory from Fear to Love, and hence Releases the Low Vibration that is Attached to that Memory from the Physical Body. An example of this could Be a Memory of the Physical Human's childhood where they were judged by a school friend that made them Feel Emotions such as Fear of Loss, Anger and Loss of Hope. With new Understanding a Truth could Be Created for that Experience such as "The Truth is that boy at school didn't hate me he was just Angry at himself". This Truth would specifically Relabel the related Memory for that Experience from Fear to Love in The Subconscious Mind of that Physical Human, due to the new Loving Understanding about that Experience. This Truth however, would not have Been Strong enough to Relabel the related Conscious Mind Perspective Programming Messages that would also link that childhood Experience at school, and that would Be Referenced by The Conscious Mind Perspective Programming multiple other Times when that Physical Human Felt judged by friends or perhaps Family or Work colleagues.

Because of this The Conscious Mind Perspective Programming would still potentially 'Perceive' Fear in other situations where in the Future the Physical Human was with friends, Family or Work colleagues and where there was a Probability of them Being judged in some way, despite the fact they would have Relabelled the child-hood Experience to 'Love' in their Subconscious Mind.

The way The Conscious Mind Perspective Programming comes into Alignment with The Subconscious Mind over 'Fear of Being Judged', is by that Physical Human over a sustained period of Time Continuously choosing Love in those situations where they still have Perceived Fear of Being Judged. Eventually if the Physical Human, despite The Conscious Mind Perspective Programming Perceiving Fear, chooses each Time to Act with Love, The Conscious Mind Perspective Programming will Relabel all Perspective Messages related to these types of situations from Fear to Love, and hence they would only Perceive Love and not Fear in these situations. This is essentially what Step Five of The Believe Releasing Process is looking to Achieve when it states 'Live your Truths'.

Now Understanding this, let us turn our attention to that Non Physical Human Now Transitioning and Going through Full Acceptance. Let us assume that they never chose Love and Lived those Truths about not Fearing Judgement when they were Physical, or perhaps that they didn't even get as far as Creating the Truth "The Truth is that boy at school didn't hate me he was just Angry at himself" during their Physical Life. They Now Find themselves in a situation where due to The Acceptance Process they Must Now Fully Accept a new Understanding and Truth for their set of related Messages around Judgement from that boy at school as well as any other Judgement from friends, Family and Work colleagues. The Acceptance Process will perhaps Focus on a series of Experiences from their Physical Life that relate to this, Connecting the Non Physical Human to different Understandings and Perspectives for each situation and Helping them to See it from a different more Loving Broader Perspective and hence Be able to Create a new Truth that in turn Relabels any 'Fear Labelled' Messages in The Conscious Mind Perspective Programming to 'Love Labelled'. This Relabelling brings them a step closer to Accepting Fully that which has gone before in their Physical Life.

This new Truth Must Be much broader than the Truth "The Truth is that boy at school didn't hate me he was just Angry at himself", this Truth is Influential in a Physical Human for Relabelling specific Memories in The Subconscious Mind but for The Conscious Mind Perspective Programming Messages, there is a link to so many other Judgement Experiences for that single Message. So, a Broader or Broadest Truth will Be brought through to the Non Physical Human that captures a much wider set of Experiences. This will Be with the Assistance of Jesus to Help Lead them to the Broader or Broadest Truth quickly, but Importantly this Truth Must Be got to by the Non Physical Human themselves in order that it Be Truly Felt and Fully Accepted by them.

An example of a Broader or Broadest Truth for the situations whereby the Non Physical Human had previously been Judged by friends, Family or Work colleagues in their Physical Life could Be "I am not a bad person", or "I am Loving", or "I don't Need to have the approval of others to Be Happy". In order for the Non Physical Human to Be able to Create any one of these three Truths they would Need to Be able to Understand more about some of the Experiences that led them to have an opposite Perspective, namely, "I am a bad person", or "I am not Loving", or "I must have the approval of others to Be Happy". And so The Acceptance Process is carefully managed by Jesus and God to bring through sufficient Understanding of other various and Important moments for the Non Physical Human from their Physical Life on Earth that Start to Build a more Loving Perspective of their Journey, Creating Broader Truths as they Understand each moment that is brought to them.

So over a period of Time the Non Physical Human will get to the position whereby they have Understood and Fully Accepted a multitude of Experiences and Journey Level Perspectives which they will have also Created Broader Truths for. The 'Broadest Truth' is the Truth that based on all of those other Understandings and Truths, Allows them to have the view that no matter what occurred in their Physical Life, the sum of all other new Broader Truths plus this specific Broadest Truth would bring them to a Place of Self Love and Full Acceptance for every Given Perspective from their Physical Life.

The Broadest Truth is similar to that of Broader Truths in that it has a Focus on a Journey Level Perspective. The key difference is that The Broadest Truth is sufficient to address all Messages in The Conscious Mind Perspective Programming that relate to the Physical Life Experiences for that Non Physical Human. To Be clear, the Broadest Truth would not Be possible for the Non Physical Human to Create without several Broader Truths Being Accepted first. So perhaps having Created the Broader Truths of "I am not a bad person", or "I am Loving", or "I don't Need to have the approval of others to Be Happy", The Broadest Truth for them could Be "Life is for Living". This Broadest Truth would have the effect of Allowing that Non Physical Human to Feel immediate Ease, a Sense of Freedom or perhaps a greater Strength and Determination to Move forward. This Broadest Truth could Be Energetically Felt at any moment of Connecting to it Consciously and immediately that Non Physical Human would Feel the Soothing from the Acceptance Energy due to the fact that they had Achieved 'Full Acceptance'.

So at this point that Full Acceptance will have been Achieved for the Non Physical Human, they Feel huge relief, as Does Jesus, God, and the Higher Self of the Non Physical Human. It Represents the moment when they can Truly Start to plan for their next stage of their Eternal Life and so with this Realisation the Non Physical Human will Start to Generate Feelings of Hope, Wonder, Enlightenment and Euphoria. What an incredible moment this is.

A Meeting With Archangel Ophelia

With Full Acceptance comes Opportunity. From years as a Physical Human Generating so much Fear, there will still Be Habitual Perspective Patterns that the Now 'Fully Accepted' Non Physical Human will need to quickly 'Break'.

We talk of 'Living Your Truths' in the Believe Releasing Process and as a Physical Human this is much more of a challenging Ask to stay Aligned to your new Truths and Live them daily amongst all of the other 'Fear Labelled' parts of Physical Life that Exist around you. But as a Non Physical Human, due to the Influence of your XFlow Lifeflow Connection keeping The Soul Balanced, and because Life in The Ethereal Realm is mainly only 'Love Labelled', Meaning it is High Vibrational, it is a much easier to Live your new Truths that have been Created.

As a Non Physical Human you can Perceive only Love, yes you can Agitate Negatively, but very quickly Agitation becomes something that occurs from the more extreme Energetic Influences that you may Experience in The Ethereal Realm. The Truths that are newly Created as part of The Full Acceptance Process will initially Be challenged as the Non Physical Human Continues to 'Reflect', Meaning that they will remember their Physical Life and Be constantly reminded of it in their interactions in The Ethereal Realm. This is because in this moment they have very few Experiences other than those from their Physical Life that they can remember, however a Meeting with Ophelia will Now Help them to 'Remember'.

To 'Remember' Means something very different to 'remember'. When you Remember you Recall those moments of your Non Physical Life and not that of your Physical Life. So for every Non Physical Human that has Started to Transition, one of the first Events that will occur after Full Acceptance is this meeting with Ophelia to Help bring them to Remember those parts of their Non Physical Life that occurred before they were a Physical Human.

Every single Human Lives in Non Physical first. They are Created by God in The Chamber Of God and they Live Life in The Ethereal Realm, and some in other Realms also. The 'Pre-Physical Life' period that they Live in Non Physical depends on their Soul Contract. For most it will Be the equivalent of around one hundred and fifty years as Experienced in Time Periods that Align to Earth 'Time and Space'. For others it can Be much quicker or even much longer. Raf and Olivia spent four thousand and fifty eight years as Souls in Non Physical before 'Transforming' to Be a Physical Human. Transforming is the process of Moving from The Ethereal Real to The Physical Realm and is a Wondrous process that 5th Dimension Earth shall discuss in Future publications.

. . .

There will Be a lot to Remember about their Pre-Physical Life for the Non Physical Human when they first Meet with Ophelia. She will Connect them to The Remembering Energy which will Be Felt in their own Chamber Of God Energetic Holding. The Non Physical Human remains in this Energy Holding for some Time and here they not only will have several conversations with Ophelia about Remembering, but they will also Be visited by old Non Physical friends and Family to Assist in the Remembering process. They will Discover that so many of their Physical Life Experiences on Earth were not only for Opportunities to Expand and Grow as a Physical Human but also Formed part of their Eternal Non Physical Journey after Transition, and were in fact part of Requests made by them to prepare them for new and exciting Possibilities in The Ethereal Realm after Transition.

The Meeting with Ophelia is one that Starts to bring great Hope to the Transitioning Non Physical Human and in particular when they Connect again with Non Physical Ancestral Souls that were part of their Physical Life on Earth. Some Transitioning Non Physical Humans will Be surprised when they Remember how Family members in their Physical Life, perhaps an aunt or uncle, were in fact some of the closest Souls to them in Non Physical Before they Transformed to Physical. These Ancestral Souls will Be brought to the Meeting by Ophelia and the Higher Self of the Non Physical Human to Share stories of their past Experiences together, both in Physical and previously in Non Physical. The Ancestors in Non Physical will perhaps also remind them of what lies ahead and how they are Going to Help them.

It is always comforting for the Non Physical Soul Going through The Transition Process to Feel that Family members in The Ethereal Realm will Be with them and supporting them for a while.

Often they can Be surprised by the role that these Non Physical Ancestral Souls Now have in Non Physical. Perhaps an auntie and uncle that were a nurse and a lorry driver in their Physical Life that were Happy just to See Life through or perhaps had many problems in their Physical Life, are Now in Non Physical great Souls and Multiversal Guides Working with Physical and Non Physical Souls across other Universes and planets, Leading the way and setting examples for All. This can Be initially Discombobulating to Understand such stark differences from when they knew them in The Physical Realm, but then as those Ancestral Souls Show them more of what they have been Working on in Non Physical and perhaps Introduce them to some of the Multiversal Souls they have been Engaging with, the Transitioning Non Physical Human Starts to Change, and with this Change comes a Soul Swell driven by the Knowing of Wondrous Opportunity for them.

Ophelia over Time will also bring to the Transitioning Non Physical Human other old Non Physical friends that they became acquainted with before they Transformed to their Physical Life. These old friends could Be Multiversal or perhaps just Souls that had Lived a Physical Life on Earth but many years before them. Perhaps these old Non Physical friends had been Guides to them when they were first Created as Non Physical Souls, Helping them to Be Ready and Learn for their Eternal Life ahead, both as a Non Physical Human and Physical Human.

All of these Interactions, together with the Balancing Influence of XFlow on their Soul, bringing a constant Perceiving of Love, as well as the ever increasing greater Understanding of their Journey that lies ahead, 'Sets' the Transitioning Non Physical Human to a new Energetic State of Knowing. This Knowing brings Acceptance that there is still so much for them to look forward to and Understand, and so this is Allowed and Felt by them, without Agitation. The Non Physical Human at this stage has a much Stronger Connection to their own Soul Energy. Ophelia will have brought to them confirmation of other Elements of their Soul Energy such as 'Key Aspects' and 'Soul Images' that Define them, their 'Soul State Of Being' that Influence the way they Act and Interact, as well as their 'Emotional Signature' which they will Now constantly Feel and which will play a huge role in the way that they Undertake everything that they as a Non Physical Human Continue to Do. Ophelia will spend a lot of Time explaining to them the Understanding as to why all of these Soul Energy Elements Form part of their Soul and how these Soul Elements were specifically Chosen by God and their own Higher Self to Align to The Soul Contract that was Desired for them, and which they themselves then later Accepted and Formed into further detail.

With all of this greater Understanding comes a Vision of why they 'Are' and with this comes Desire, Hope and Aspiration. The Non Physical Human at this stage is like a race horse desperate to get out of the traps. They have been skilfully and Loving brought here by Jesus, God, their Higher Self and of course Ophelia. It has Taken huge Courage from the Non Physical Human to Fully Accept all that has gone before in their Physical Life, good and bad.

Now the Non Physical Human is almost Ready to Transition.

This Non Physical Human is Strong, able, Capable and Focused.

So what's left?

God

To Know God the way Raf and Olivia Do, 5th Dimension Earth will look forward to clarifying and also publishing further on. His different Energies, 'The Solution of God', how God was Created and the Understanding that before God, came God. God's Highest State. There are so many areas to Understand and these will Lovingly Be brought through by God at the Right Time for all Physical Humans.

But for Non Physical Humans, the Right Time is at the point where they are Ready to Fully Transition. The answer to so many of the questions that the Non Physical Human may have Asked as a Physical Human will Be Given to them at this Time. The Non Physical Human will also Feel in this meeting with God a Unique Energy as they talk with each other about this. This Energy is God's History. All that had gone before for God in this moment is Now Felt by the Non Physical Human. This Energy of History is so much more than the dictionary definition of the word History. For the Spiritual Reference 'History' Represents past Probability, but also Now and the Future and the Possibility that comes with this to make new Probability. It is in this Energy of God's History that the Non Physical Human 'Knows'. Knows what has occurred trillions of years before and what will occur trillions of years into the Future, and beyond, Eternally. This Knowing is not bringing through information on the Future of Earth, or the latest gadgets that Physical Humans will Be Using, or whether green men in suits are Going to visit in space ships. No, this Knowing is about Love.

A Love so Strong that it will momentarily Light up the Non Physical Human, and in this Lighting will come a Truth. Not The Broadest Truth. This Truth is All encompassing. It's a Truth that just makes everything Clear. This Truth is 'The Truth Of God'. A simple Truth that just 'Is'.

And when this simple Truth 'Is' for the Non Physical Human nothing else Needs to Be explained.

"And so Now, Transition Complete".

13

GRANITTE ENERGY

Granitte is an Energy that is Created by anyone that has Activated The Christ Consciousness Gateway. It is most commonly Created therefore when someone Commences Transition after their Physical Death. Granitte is however also Created when a Physical Human Soul Activates The Christ Consciousness Gateway but then Returns to The Physical Realm.

Granitte Energy is among the most Ethereal of Energies and is an Energy that is Used and reUsed by those in Non Physical but that is also available to Be Used and reUsed by Physical Humans that are Expanded sufficiently at their Inner Being Level.

The 'Profile' of the Granitte Energy is Unique for every 'Insertion'. An Insertion Represents an individual instance of Granitte Energy that is Created by a specific Soul. An Insertion will occur only once for each moment that The Christ Consciousness Gateway is Activated by a Soul. There will Be some Physical Humans that will

Activate The Christ Consciousness Gateway several Times in a Sequence due to Experiencing the Possibility of Death in multiple Moments, for example a Physical Human that is Fighting to Live can often Activate The Christ Consciousness Gateway several Times as they battle to remain in The Physical Realm. In this example the Physical Human will 'Insert' new Granitte Energy for every separate Activation of The Christ Consciousness Gateway, and as every single Activation will Represent a different Experience, each Inserted Granitte Energy will Be Unique and separate.

Granitte Energy is the Energy of Experience in The Christ Consciousness Gateway. There are Non Physical Souls that can deliberately Intend to Activate The Christ Consciousness Gateway and in Doing so they too will Insert a Unique Granitte Energy. This is a common activity for the more Expanded and Higher Dimensional Non Physical Souls, for the Energy of Granitte can Be so valuable in Creation and Co-Creation, and so that Expanded Non Physical Soul will Be specific about their activities when they Activate The Christ Consciousness Gateway in order to define the Profile of the Granitte Energy Insertion.

The simplicity and Purity of Granitte Energy is the Reason for its incredible Capability and Influence. Granitte Energy is 'Attached to' and cannot Be Harnessed or Leveraged as is the case in other Energetic Law combined Energetic Interactions. When a Unique Granitte Energy Profile is Needed it is 'Located' and the Attachment to it comes from the other Energy Types that will Form part of the overall new Energetic Configuration for the proposed Purpose of that new Energetic Configuration and Energy Type that contains the 'Attached to' Granitte Energy. The 'Location' for Granitte is in the Unique Energetic Holding of The Chamber Of God for the Physical Human Soul that the Granitte was Inserted by. The Reference to 'Inserted' describes the Ownership that is Given to the Human Soul from which the Granitte Energy was Formed and which then was immediately and permanently Allocated to their own Chamber Of God Energetic Holding. It is in this specific and permanent Allocating that the Granitte Energy is Deemed Inserted there, and therefore to Use or reUse any Granitte Energy the Creator of it Must always Set Intention to 'Allow' its Use or reUse when Asked.

The Possibilities for Use and reUse of Granitte Energy are far reaching. Granitte Energy 'Submits' when combined with other Energy Types. It Submits to whatever the Intention is Given by the Creator wanting to Create the combined new Energy Type Configuration. By Submitting, the Granitte Energy Forms part of whatever is Needed Energetically by Interacting and Allowing itself to evolve and Change, but also if required, it Influences the other Energy Types by Encouraging the Energies with which it is to Be combined with, to Align to it and therefore Change in Type or Profile themselves. It Takes much Learning and Understanding of Granitte Energy before a Human Soul can properly Work with it, however once Known it is through mere Intention that the Human Soul can combine and Form the greatest of new Energies with it. This is because Granitte Energy is Understood and Learnt through Soul Exercising and therefore once The Soul Knowing on how to Create new Energy Types from Granitte Energy is in Place, The Soul of the Human that has Learnt can then Apply Intention to Create whatever combined Energy Type is Needed from the Granitte Energy and the Forming and Inserting of this will then Be Continued Unconsciously.

The Use and ReUse of Granitte Energy for Physical Healing are the most common, for example the Higher Self of a Soul having a

Physical Life can Extend to that Physical Human the Capability to Influence their Physical Cells to Heal. The range of this Healing Capability is dependent on the Granitte Energy but also the Energetic Capability of the Higher Self and also the Inner Being Levels of the Physical Human Being Healed.

The Granitte Energy of some of the most Wondrous Interactions in The Christ Consciousness Gateway has also been Attached to in order to Create new combined Energy Types that bring the Capability for the most Wondrous Soul Knowing Exchanges. A Granitte Energy Attached to a new Energetic Type and Capability that brings Soul Knowing can Exercise The Soul in such a way that it brings to The Conscious Mind Perspective Programming or Consciousness Perspective, Understanding of the original Granitte Energy Experience. In this scenario the Granitte Energy cannot provide the actual Memory of Experience for this is 'Washed' when the Granitte Energy is originally Formed and Inserted, however The Soul Knowing within the Granitte Energy for that Experience can Trigger new Understanding when a certain Perspective is Taken by the Physical Human or Non Physical Human Soul. So when a specific Perspective is Perceived by the recipient of the new Energy Type containing the Granitte Energy, The Soul Knowing from the Granitte Energy original Experience Held in the new Energy Type, in that moment of that specific Perceiving for the Human, Exercises their Soul and as a Consequence, that Soul Understands and even Forms their own Memory or Perspective of the Understanding from the specific original Experience Held within the Granitte Energy. With this Flows Feeling and a Cognitive Sense of what that Soul Knowing relates to within Granitte Energy original Experience, and hence in this moment comes a wonderful Opportunity to Share that Experience with Love and Insight, and to Learn and evolve from it without having Experienced it themselves.

. . .

Consider The Soul Knowing Possibilities from a situation of mass Death, perhaps from a single event or over an Elongated period due to war or disease. Non Physical Humans have often Formed new Energy Types by combining and Attaching to the Granitte Energies of those Souls that have Activated The Christ Consciousness Gateway on a large scale together, and combined all of their Granitte Energy to Form a single new Energy Type to Create something Wondrous for those Souls that they may have left behind in The Physical Realm. Imagine Attaching to the Granitte Energy of all of those Souls that would have Shared Death at the same Time that were then Guided by Jesus in The Christ Consciousness Gateway to Feel Hope that they are Now Commencing their Eternal Life, to Feel Faith that God Exists and who Loves them so, and Being Soothed by Jesus in the Understanding that those in The Physical Realm that they have left behind will Soon Be with them again. This beautiful collection of Granitte Energy from those Souls who have Activated The Christ Consciousness Gateway on mass together could Be Used by all of the Higher Selves of those Loved Ones that are still Physical and that will no doubt Be suffering greatly at the Death of so many Physical Humans that they also Loved. This new Energy Type Using the multiple and combined Granitte Energy would bring a Soul Knowing to those Physical Humans left behind by those Souls that had on mass Died and Commenced Transition, and this would bring so much more than just Emotional Soothing. The Higher Selves of those Physical Humans would Extend to them the new Energy Type consisting of the multiple Granitte Energies from those that had Died, and this would bring the Cognitive Soul Understanding for them that those Souls that on mass had Experienced Death were Going to Continue Living Eternally, that they were not suffering greatly and that they Soon would Be together with them again.

. . .

This of course would not completely remove the Grief and Emotional pain that those Physical Humans that were left behind would Be Going through after such an Experience, but so often it has been the case that when Using Granitte Energy for this Purpose that it would Be enough for those Physical Humans to just keep Living their own Physical Lives, to Find a way to get through their own distress and to Connect to Love and Hope that Life will get better for them.

The Use and reUse of Granitte Energy between Non Physical Souls is a constant activity and Forms part of evolvement of Non Physical Capability for Non Physical Humans, Helping them to Expand and Grow in line with their own Eternal Soul Contract Definitions and aspirations.

For Non Physical Souls, the Using and reUsing of Granitte Energy brings a greater Connection to Physical Humans and in particular the Higher Self Souls and their Physical Human Incarnations. A Higher Self cannot Physically Incarnate at this Time and so in Using or reUsing Granitte Energy Inserted by a Physical Human Allows the Higher Self to Understand so much more about how the Physical Human Soul is Influenced by the challenges of a Physical Human Life, and also how those challenges are overcome. As well as personal Learning for the Higher Self, this Use or reUse of Granitte Energy in this way can Help them when Working with newly Created Souls in their Soul Contract Definitions. Often a new Soul in Non Physical that is preparing for a Physical Life will want to challenge themselves greatly for their ultimate Expansion, and because of this they often Ask for the most difficult of Experiences to Be Defined as 'Pre-Manifested Events' in their Soul Contract in order to Achieve this. It is the role of their Higher Self as well as God to Try to Balance these challenging aspirations with the Truth of how some of those Asked for Experiences may cause great suffering for them in their Physical Life, and therefore a Higher Self that themselves has a Soul Knowing of a particular Experience through the Use of Granitte Energy Inserted by a Soul that will have had a similar Experience in their Physical Human Life, can Enable themselves to better Guide on the merits and difficulties that may Be faced for that Soul wishing to Define that Physical Experience in their Soul Contract for their Physical Life. In Doing so they perhaps persuade them to Change or soften that specific Soul Contract Ask in order that Physical Life may Be more Balanced for them.

The Higher Self can also 'Extend' any Soul Knowing that they will have Achieved through Working with a specific Granitte Energy to another Soul that may also Need to Understand The Soul Knowing provided by the specific Granitte Energy. If the Intended recipient of The Soul Knowing is sufficiently Expanded to Receive it, this is Undertaken without that other Soul having to Work directly with the Granitte Energy as the Knowing has already been Understood by the Higher Self Soul who will Unconsciously Undertake the Work required to Exercise The Soul of the recipient. Again this is common between Highly Ascended Non Physical Souls, however it has also been Undertaken regularly with Physical Human Souls that have Expanded sufficiently their Inner Being Levels whilst Living their Physical Human Life.

Whilst it is Possible as a Non Physical Human to Insert Granitte Energy by specifically Activating The Christ Consciousness Gateway to Do so, it is the Granitte Energy of a Physical Human that has Activated The Christ Consciousness Gateway that is the most Influential when Using and reUsing.

The Granitte Energy of a Physical Human captures the Physical Energy of the Third Dimension, hence it has a strong Physical Energy Sequencing to it and this makes it a particularly potent Energy. This potency Ensures a much greater Influence when Forming the new Energy Type from the particular Granitte Energy or Energies. It is therefore the Granitte Energy that is Inserted by a Physical Human that has Activated The Christ Consciousness Gateway that is most commonly combined and configured into new Energy Types that would Be Used or reUsed for broader requirements where perhaps multiple Souls or All Souls would benefit from a single newly configured Energy Type. A single Granitte Energy from a single Physical Human can Be so Influential on the many as is it commonly full of so much Love and that Love which is Attached to a Physical Sequencing has the greatest of potency and Influence for All when Used or reUsed as a new Energy Type.

It is the Capture of the Third Dimensional Physical Energy Sequences that makes Granitte Energy so Powerful and hence the Reason why Granitte Energy Insertion was made Possible by God. Whilst the Granitte Energy previously Created by a Physical Human Soul can Be Used and reUsed by other Souls when Allowed, due to Energetic Law, the Granitte Energy of a Physical Human Soul that is still Living a Physical Life cannot Be reconfigured into a new Energy Type. Hence only in the moments when a Living Physical Human Soul Creates a Non Physical Energy (such as that Created when they Activate The Christ Consciousness Gateway), can their Granitte Energy Form a new Energy Type configuration.

. . .

There are infinite Possibilities of what a single Granitte Energy Insertion can contain and this will Be something that 5th Dimension Earth will provide further information on in Future publications. The Purpose of Introducing Granitte Energy in this book was to Understand a most wonderful element of The Christ Consciousness Gateway Activation and indeed Transition Commencement. At this most difficult of Times for many Physical Humans where they face Death or potential Death it is Important to Understand that the Physical Life of that Soul is already Starting to Influence All when they Commence Transition. For in the Using and reUsing of their Granitte Energy Inserted by them, God has Given Opportunities for so much Expansion and Ascension across the Multiverse. The Forming and Inserting of Granitte Energy by a Physical Human Soul in these difficult moments within The Christ Consciousness Gateway brings something so Ethereal, so Precious and so appreciated by those Non Physical Souls already in The Ethereal Realm, for they Know what Granitte Energy Represents from that Physical Life Journey of the Physical Human. They Know how Courageous the Physical Human will have been during their Physical Life and what that then would have brought to that Granitte Energy, and they will Know just how Influential that Granitte Energy will Be, Eternally.

14

FLOW

There is a Statement that Archangel Ophelia Gives to every Non Physical Soul on completion of The Acceptance Process.

Love. Live. Flow.

We wish to Focus on 'Flow'. For Flow is something that Physical Humans are Masterful with when they Acknowledge it Exists and then Allow themselves to Find it consistently. When Physical Humans Find Flow their Soul Energy Agitates in numerous different ways, and always Lovingly.

For Non Physical Humans, Flow comes upon the completion of Transition. A Non Physical Soul that has Transitioned is in the moment of Achieving it, configured by XFlow to Energetically Flow at all Times. Yes, they will occasionally Agitate Negatively from High Frequency High Vibrational Influences, and on occasion due to negative Influences that they Allow, perhaps from Sensing a Loved One suffering in The Physical Realm, but these Negative Agitations will never Stop them from Flowing.

Flow is a 'Spiritual Function' Reference and is something that is 'Known' by all Souls for all Physical Human and Non Physical Soul Model Types. When Flow is Felt by The Soul, it 'Is'. Flow always 'Is' with Non Physical Humans that have Transitioned and hence they will always Feel a Sense of it. Flow is Felt by Non Physical Humans as a Continuous Movement of Energy, and depending on what other Influences are occurring with the Non Physical Human, Flow will Be either Consciously Understood or Unconsciously Allowed, or both.

Think of Flow not simply as an Energy but as Law. Flow is 'Weaved' into so many Elements of Life in Non Physical, not just Humans, but 'All'. Flow is Designed to bring Alignment to all that it Weaves through and hence a Physical Human or Non Physical Human that Flows Ensures they are exactly where they Must Be Energetically in each moment, Aligned to themselves and therefore The Self, for it is Correct that all Humans Must Flow, as it is an Important Reference for them in 'The Truth Of You'.

Flow is something that the Non Physical Human can Be temporarily Shifted from Feeling, but will never Be Removed from. Flow is not something that the Non Physical Human Needs to Go looking for, unlike Physical Humans who Need to make a more Conscious effort to Find Flow when they Shift from it.

·   ·   ·

This Capability to always Flow Means that that Non Physical Humans Live very much in Now. Even when Actively Ubiquitous they are 'Consciously Present' of all that they are Energetically Engaged with. This is made possible through their Unconscious Gateway and Eternal Lifeflow that Acts as the Conduit to all Ubiquity for them. In an Active State of Ubiquity the Non Physical Human could Find themselves Being Influenced in different ways Energetically from differing Energies in the various locations that they are Encountering. All of these will Be Sensed and Felt separately but there will still always remain an overriding Flow in The Soul of the Non Physical Human.

This permanence of Flow Ensures that the Non Physical Human not only stays Balanced but also Notices so much more, and specifically the Love that Surrounds them. In this Noticing of Love they are Encouraged to Generate more 'Love Labelled' Energy themselves. It is Flow that always brings a Non Physical Human back to Love and Self Love, and it really is one of the most powerful Energies that Exist because of this.

Flow also Acts with positive 'Kinetic Influence', Meaning it drives positive Energy into that in which it 'Is'. For a Non Physical Human the positive Kinetic Influence is both on The Soul Energy as well as their Consciousness Perspective. The Soul benefits from the perpetual 'Love Labelled' Influence on it, constantly Being Agitated with Love and because of this it brings an Attraction of more Love to the Non Physical Human. This Circle Of Love also Continuously brings a positive Soul Swell to the Non Physical Human and Importantly Allows them to keep Focused to 'Feel Good'. The Consciousness Perspective of the Non Physical Human also benefits from the positive Kinetic Influence in that it Ensures less Negative Infiltration and Helps bring Clarity of Thought and

Balance. All of these positive Influences combine to Allow the Non Physical Human to function optimally at the maximum Energetic Capacity for 'The Self' and hence perform to the best of their Capabilities, and again, Importantly, FEEL GOOD.

'The Self' for a Physical Human consists of The Soul Energy, The Physical Body, The Emotional Body, The Egoic Bodies, The Energetic Minds that consist of The Conscious Mind, The Conscious Mind Perspective Programming, The Subconscious Mind and The Unconscious Mind (for more information on the Emotional Body and The Egoic Bodies, please reference the 5th Dimension Earth book Believe). For a Non Physical Human, The Self consists of The Soul Energy, Consciousness Perspective and The Unconscious.

When The Self is Aligned to itself, in other words all Elements that Define it are in Alignment, the Physical Human or Non Physical Human 'Flows'. For a Physical Human it is mainly the Physical Body and The Mind that come out of Alignment and therefore what Stops them Flowing. A Non Physical Human never comes out of Alignment to The Self and this is because they Flow permanently. Flow is what Ensures that as a Non Physical Human Eternally Expands and Grows their Soul, the other Elements of The Self don't get out of Alignment. For example, if a Non Physical Human Undertakes Energetic Ability Exercising and Enactment of The Soul Energy, their Inner Being will Expand to new Levels and it is likely that their Knowing Level will also Ascend and during this period, as they are always in Flow, The Consciousness Perspective and The Unconscious for them remains Aligned and hence The Self is also always Aligned, and this Expansion and Ascension brings an immediate positive Energetic Consequence for the Non Physical Human. If a Physical Human was Energetically Expanding their Inner Being and Ascending their Knowing

Levels, perhaps through an Awakening, it is highly likely that for a period of Time The Self would come out of Alignment (assuming it was in Alignment previously). This is because through the greater Soul Knowing and Energetic Capability would come greater Energetic Expectation on The Energetic Minds as well as The Physical Body for them, Possibly due to Interaction with differing Energy Types, considering The Soul's increased Energetic Capability. This new Energetic Expectation and Understanding would not come automatically to The Energetic Minds, particularly The Conscious Mind Perspective Programming, nor to the Physical Body, and this would bring Discombobulation and misAlignment of The Self for that Physical Human, and hence the Capability to Take full advantage of their Soul Energy Expansion and Knowing Level Ascension would also Be lessened considerably in the short term.

For Non Physical Humans there would Be no such Alignment Interruption, as Flow, through the XFlow Function of the Non Physical Human, would always Ensure that The Self Expands their Soul Energy, Consciousness Perspective and The Unconscious together. If the Non Physical Soul Energy Expands and Ascends Knowing Levels it cannot Do so without Ensuring that The Consciousness Perspective and The Unconscious are Capable of Interpreting and Using the increased Soul Capabilities and Knowing that have come about from The Soul Energy Expansion and Knowing Ascension. Without this, Soul Energetic Capability would also remain unUsed or unable to Be Harnessed or Leveraged by the Non Physical Human. For example, Consciousness Perspective could become unable to Interpret new Soul Energetic Capability and this would Create a 'Reluctance' Energetically. Think of Energetic Reluctance as a Kinetic slowing down whereby Understanding would not able to Be Interpreted by The Consciousness Perspective about something that The Soul is able to Know. This could Be something as simple as a Soul Contract Milestone for the Non Physical Human that had been newly Created due to broader circumstances in The Soul Contracts of others, and which ultimately Influenced their own Soul Contract. You may question why the Insertion of a new Soul Contract Milestone would not Be able to Be Interpreted by the Non Physical Human's Consciousness Perspective, even though it is 'Known' by their Soul. It is actually a simple point to clarify. The Energy around the Entry for that new Soul Contract Milestone is Registered based on a specific Energetic Understanding brought about by the new Soul Knowing, and with this new Energetic Understanding comes Influence from new and specific Energy Types for that Non Physical Human. Without The Consciousness Perspective also having the Capability to Interpret those new Energy Types, the Thoughts of the Non Physical Human would become Discombobulated when Trying to Consciously Interpret what The Soul 'Knows' and Understands, and hence they would begin to Infiltrate Incorrectly with Conscious Interpretation over the matter that they were wishing to Interpret from the new Soul Knowing. Ultimately this would Mean an Incorrect Consciousness Perspective Understanding over that which The Soul Knows about the new Soul Contract Milestone.

It is rare, but this scenario could also occur for a Physical Human that had 'greatly' Expanded their Inner Being and Ascension Levels to a point where their Conscious Mind Perspective Programming is unable to Interpret a new Soul Knowing, and this could also extend to The Physical Body whereby The Soul was Asking The Physical Body, via The Conscious Mind Perspective Programming 'Cellular Understanding', to Undertake certain Cellular Functions that it had never Been previously Requested to Undertake. For example, due to new Soul Energy Knowing, the Cells of the Physical Human may Be Receiving new Cellular

Command Sets linked to highly advanced Physical Healing, but without the Capability of The Conscious Mind Perspective Programming to Interpret this information Received from The Soul, that Cellular Command Set could not Be Directed to the Cells and therefore the new Physical Healing Energy Received by The Soul because of its Expanded and Ascended Capability, could not Be Taken advantage of by the Physical Human, until The Self of the Physical Human was able to Align all Capability across The Soul Energy, The Energetic Minds and the Physical Body over Time. This could be driven by further Expansion of the Physical Human that brought their Conscious Mind Perspective Programming as well as perhaps Cellular Memory Capability, into line with their previous Soul Energy Expansion and Knowing Ascension. A Physical Human that has Experienced great Inner Being Expansion and Knowing Ascension may also Find their Unconscious Mind immediately becomes out of Alignment and in so Doing, for the Physical Human, they will get a Sense of increased Knowing but without the Cognitive Ability to Feel it to Be True, again something that the Non Physical Human will not Experience as they will always Flow and hence will always have an Alignment to The Self.

The constant Alignment of The Self for Non Physical Humans is critical considering the huge amount of Soul Expansion that occurs for them in The Ethereal Realm, and this is why Flow is 'Assured' for all Non Physical Humans, once Transition is Complete. However, for a newly Transitioning Soul this Alignment of The Self is not instant. Consider that they have come from a Physical Human Soul Model whereby The Self is usually not Aligned. When they Complete Transition, Flow will Start the process of looking to Align The Self i.e. their Unconsciousness, their Consciousness Perspective and their Non Physical Soul Energy, which as part of the Transition Process Completion Must immediately Be fully able to Translate with the Energy Types that it Needs to within The Ethereal Realm. However as part of Full Acceptance during the Transition Process and whilst they are therefore still Transitioning, the Non Physical Human's Soul still Needs to Hold a Perspective Understanding Capability from their Life as a Physical Human and hence they Must only have Capability to Interpret with the same Energy Types that their Soul Energy Interacted with whilst they were a Physical Human. This Hold on Energy Type Interpretation remains in Place until after Transition Complete for the Non Physical Human. The Conscious Mind Perspective Programming will not immediately Be Aligned to that which their Non physical Soul is Now Starting to Know from their brief Time in The Ethereal Realm, and hence The Self for the Transitioning Non Physical Human at this point is not Aligned. This has an Energetic effect on the Non Physical Human that is similar to when a vinyl record Being played gets the needle of the record player stuck on it, repeating the same part of the song over and over. Flow in a similar way in this moment is looking to Move Understanding of new Soul Knowing for the Transitioning Non Physical Human into Alignment with their Conscious Mind Perspective Programming, but The Conscious Mind Perspective Programming from their Physical Life is not Designed to Translate correctly with the same Energy Types as can Be Interacted with in The Ethereal Realm and so the newly Transitioning Non Physical Human will have moments where they Discombobulate and Feel out of Balance and not Flowing. Flow will Continue to Try to Energetically Move The Self for that Transitioning Non Physical Human into Alignment, and this will Be Vibrationally Felt, Seen, Heard or Known by the Non Physical Soul constantly until it is Possible to Do so. It is this constant Move to bring The Self into Alignment during this Transitioning period that brings 'the needle stuck on the vinyl record' effect for the Non Physical Human as the Energy Request from Flow Repeats over and over in a way that will Be Felt, Seen, Heard or

Known by them. Whilst this Discombobulation Continuously occurs during The Transition Process it Acts as a reminder to the Non Physical Human of Flow, for they will Be able to Interpret that Flow is looking to Align The Self and in Doing so Feel more Assured during the process of Transition. Once the Non Physical Human Fully Transitions The Self is able to 'Acknowledge' all the Non Physical Interactions and therefore Flow in this moment, via the Non Physical Human's 'XFlow Lifeflow' will Start the process of Allowing the necessary Changes that are required to Align. This requires no Interaction by the Non Physical Human as Flow and XFlow Work together to Understand where Alignment Needs to occur.

All of this Alignment Work for the newly Transitioned Non Physical Human will still initially cause them an increased Energetic Output even with a permanent Flow in Place, as they Focus on Flowing and Noticing the Energetic Requests from Flow in order to Move into Alignment. Their Higher Self will Assist in this process, and this is also something that Archangel Ophelia will also have provided Guidance on during the Full Acceptance Process. The Non Physical Human Goes through a period of Energetic Distress and Agitation during Full Acceptance through to Transition Complete and Work will also Continue for them after Transition to find Balance and to Ensure that they quickly become Capable of a far greater independence in their Eternal Non Physical Life in The Ethereal Realm.

With this independence comes great Opportunity and Possibility, and the Start of the next Phase of their Soul Contract where they are Free to evolve and Grow as they wish. Soon after this Follows new aspirations for the Non Physical Human, new Interactions, a new Non Physical Family and hence a greater Sense of Belonging.

From this Starts the ongoing evolvement of the Non Physical Human.

It is Flow that is key to Starting this evolvement process, Assuring Alignment to The Self and in Doing so Enabling the maximum Possibility for the Non Physical Human to Live an Eternal Life of Balance and Love and Magnificence.

15

THE CHAMBER OF GOD

The Chamber Of God is an Energetic Holding of the greatest proportions in the Ethereal Realm. This Energetic Holding is the Place where every single Human, Physical and Non Physical, was Created and Born in The Ethereal Realm.

The Chamber Of God is however Unique for every single Human and hence every single Human has their own specific and personal Energetic Holding within The Chamber Of God that relates to them only. This specific Energetic Holding within The Chamber Of God is not only the Place where all Human Souls are Created and Born but also where they will spend a huge proportion of their Time before their Physical Human Life and also ongoing in their Eternal Non Physical Human Life after Transition.

The Chamber Of God is a Place where a Non Physical Human Learns so much of what they come to Understand about Life, where they evolve for Energetic Expansion with their Higher Self and other Guides, and it is also a social Place for them where they will often host other Non Physical Human Souls to simply Share how the day has gone or perhaps what Excites them about the next Phase of their Soul Contract.

The Chamber Of God is such a Place of Interaction for the Non Physical Human and because they have their own Energetic Holding within there, it is also a Place of privacy and Assurance for them to Undertake whatever it is that they so wish with themselves or others. In the same way that Physical Humans usually come home at the end of their day to where they Live, a Non Physical Human will often return to their own Energetic Holding within The Chamber Of God.

But The Chamber Of God is far more than a Place of Learning or rest or socialising, it is a Place of Love. It is a Sanctuary where so many Wondrous Energies can Be Harnessed and Felt. It is an Ethereal Place for each individual Human Soul, that contains so much of their own Energy of Creation and which can Be so Soothing for them simply to sit within. Feelings of Powerful Love, Peace and other harmonious Vibrations are Held there and specifically Placed there by Intention to Be Enjoyed. It's rather like hanging framed photos of your children or your favourite painting around your house to Enjoy, the Energy that is Held permanently within your own Unique Energy Holding within The Chamber Of God very much Represents you and what you will have Energetically Placed there.

The Chamber Of God and your specific Energetic Holding also 'Keeps' an Energy of past Experiences there. The Memories from these Experiences will also Be Remembered if Connected to but it is the Experiences themselves that Keep a permanent Energy within your Chamber Of God Energetic Holding. The Experience of first meeting with God at your Non Physical Time of Being Born, the moments you Lovingly Shared with an Eternal Soul Pair Relationship, Time spent with Ancestral Souls or other Soul Group friends laughing and having so much Enjoyment with them, conversations with your Higher Self, and of course those Wondrous other moments with God. All of this is there, Felt and Consciously recallable for even greater Energetic fulfilment.

Your Energetic Holding within The Chamber Of God will Hold an Energetic Record of your Expansion and Ascension through Soul Knowing Levels. These are actual Energetic Registered Entries, rather like a library or a shelf of Important books or documents that you keep in your home, these Registered Entries are a Confirmation of your Journey, not of specific Experiences but rather of Achievements. These Achievements could Be from specific Energetic Capabilities that have been Enabled, how they were Exercised and which other Souls Helped you to Achieve them, or Influenced you in some way to Achieve them. It is also a Place where you can Energetically Record personal information, rather like a log or a diary, you can Record Freely your own thoughts and Perspectives on any matter or Experience and it is an extremely valuable source of Information and History that you will often refer to or discuss with your Higher Self or God or perhaps others Souls that you are Working with on specific Energetic activities.

As a Physical Human it is Possible to 'Remember Episodes' from your Chamber Of God Energetic Holding. This would Be Experiences and moments that you can Connect to Using the Remembering Energy. This can Be one of the most Amazing and Freeing of Experiences as a Non Physical Human. Moments such as your last meeting with your Higher Self or God Before Transforming to your Physical Life, or a Time when you would have been with your Soul Group Family Sharing Love and Understanding and Connection with them, those Souls that would Be Parents or Siblings in your Physical Life and that would perhaps Be Disconnected from you as your Physical Family in your Physical Life. If Connected to when you are Physical Human, something as simple as Remembering an Exchange in Non Physical within The Chamber Of God, that can Be the catalyst for Change and Acceptance and a new way forward with them in your Physical Life, merely by Remembering the True relationship with them from your Non Physical Time spent together.

For a Physical Human, a Connection to your specific Chamber Of God Energetic Holding can also bring Physical Healing. As a Non Physical Human you will have Created so much that was new Energetically there, that was also very specific to you as a Non Physical Human Soul, but also in readiness for your Physical Human Life. You will have Understood your Soul Contract and how it may Manifest as a Physical Human and you will have been specifically Guided by many other Non Physical Guides about this and how to prepare for your Physical Life. It is not uncommon for the Non Physical Human to deliberately Create Energy that 'Matches' that of their own Soul Energy and which can then Be Leveraged or Harnessed by them for later Soul Energy Expansion. This Matched Energy could then Be Used to Exercise their Soul in a way that developed new Physical Human or Non Physical Human Capabilities or just Helped to evolve Existing ones. The Chamber Of God is a space where literally for themselves, anything can Be attempted and commonly is by the Non Physical Human. It is their personal Place of Intention and Possibility and aspiration.

. . .

As a Physical Human, Knowing that there is Unique Energy in your Chamber Of God Energetic Holding that Matches your Soul, it is Possible to Intend to reUse that Energy of Creation for yourself in your Physical Life on Earth. A Matched Healing Energy 'Knows' your Soul, it can Feel your Alignment or Discombobulation as a Physical Human and it is as simple as just Allowing Matched Healing Energy for you as a Physical Human to Receive Physical Healing from it. You will Need to firstly Connect to your Unique Energy Holding in The Chamber Of God but then no more would Need to Be Undertaken other than to Start the Intention to Allow the Matched Healing Energy that Exists there. Matched Healing Energy can Be Received by you in a way that would Be Energetically more Influential than many other Energies you will have Allowed. Because of this the positive Consequences for you are dramatically greater than most other Physical Healing Energies that you could ever Experience, and the Physical Body Healing results for you as a Physical Human can also Be breathtaking, simply because of the Matched Interaction with your own Soul Energy that could not Be replicated by the Healing Energy of most other Souls or Non Physical Entities that you may Accept Physical Healing from.

The Chamber Of God for an individual Soul is a Magnificent Energetic Holding. As a Transitioning Non Physical Human, The Chamber Of God is where you will meet with Archangel Ophelia as part of The Full Acceptance Process. As has been discussed in the chapter on The Transition Process, it is the Energetic space chosen for this meeting as it will contain so much that is familiar to you, and the Energy of Love and Assurance that you will have previously Created there will Help to bring the Transitioning Non Physical Human to a Place of Balance as they Start Life after Death. They will quickly Remember Experiences from their Non Physical Life prior to Transforming to a Physical Human, especially when some old Non Physical friends Show up and Start reminding them of some of their past Experiences in Non Physical with them. These meetings with old friends are moments of Wonder for those Non Physical Souls that are Asked to come and support you through the Full Acceptance Process of Transition. To Be Present in your Chamber Of God Energetic Holding during this Time is a privilege Held in such high regard and something that is so special to them, and so the Love that is Generated at this Time by all that come to support and Guide the Transitioning Non Physical Human is Immense. The Energy of this Experience with Archangel Ophelia and those Asked to Be part of Full Acceptance is something that is Eternally Held there and Continually Connected to by many Non Physical Humans in the periods shortly after their Full Transition, for those Energies Represent a Knowing that they are so Loved and that so much Love Exists in The Ethereal Realm, and this brings Balance and Hope for them through these earlier moments after Transition.

The Chamber Of God will Eternally Be a space of Discovery for the Non Physical Human after Transition. The Chamber Of God Energetic Holding for that Non Physical Human Soul provides a point of Connection and 'Bridges' to so many other parts of The Ethereal Realm and also into other Realms. Your specific Energetic Holding within The Chamber Of God can Open itself to Connection to other Universes and therefore other Human relationships and encounters. The Chamber Of God also provides Protection from those Energies that the Non Physical Human has yet to fully Understand and that therefore could Discombobulate or Agitate them. It is an incredible Energetic Holding that Allows Assured Interaction and Learning with new and Exciting Energies, Human or otherwise, that will Help to develop the Non Physical Human on their ongoing Eternal Journey in a way that Ensures no negative Influences, and hence Expansion and Knowing Ascension with Love.

This is the Wonder of The Chamber Of God. It is a personal Energetic space for All with so much Possibility to evolve just quietly alone, or with a group of close Non Physical friends or Guides, but also with so many Opportunities to Open up to 'All That Is' and to Enjoy the Magic that comes with those Multiversal Interactions. The Chamber Of God is one of the greatest Achievements of God, Designed to Create Love in Abundance and to Be the greatest of Influences for Creation and Co-Creation. For the newly Transitioned Soul it is literally Life Changing and it so quickly can Move them from the Agitation of what they have left behind from their Physical Life on Earth, to then Lead them to the most Magnificent of Eternal Journeys for themselves and others.

16

CAN YOU HEAR THE LOVE

'Can You Hear The Love'. Not a question but another Spiritual Term. A Spiritual Term that Relates to Ethereal Understanding for those that have Allowed Full Acceptance after Transition.

So what Does this Spiritual Term Align to and effectively Mean? It's actually easier to Understand if you Try and Connect to this Spiritual Term as an Energy that you can Feel. As a Physical Human it will not Be possible to Feel the Energy of this Term but we can attempt to Help you to get a Sense of it.

You Feel Hope. You Feel an Importance around Love and Need to Act with Love and Self Love. You get a Connection to your own Importance and Energetic Soul Capability and Influence and this brings a Balance, a Desire and a Flow.

.   .   .

The Spiritual Term 'Can You Hear The Love' is also a 'Recognition Statement' from God which Asks you to Understand the Feeling that this Term brings you as a Transitioned Non Physical Human. For this Feeling brings you to 'Recognise' your Eternalness, your True Energy and a Sense of your Soul Purpose and Meaning. Your Higher Self Feels your Soul Energy Flow each moment that you Recognise this Spiritual Term and in turn both you and your Higher Self Energetically Expand your Inner Being, it's Magical.

The Significance of Can You Hear The Love

This Spiritual Term is hugely significant as it can Open an Energy in you of Strength and Resilience. A newly Transitioned Non Physical Human Takes a little while to Find themselves and their Place Energetically in The Ethereal Realm. Once the initial Joy of meeting old friends and previously Transitioned Family members is Experienced it is Important to quickly 'Set' yourself and this involves Agreeing with your Higher Self your immediate Future and aspirations. The Spiritual Term 'Can You Hear The Love' Works with The Soul Energy in a way that is very specific and also personal to the newly Transitioned Non Physical Human. In this very personal Interaction with this Spiritual Term they Feel Wonder at what lies ahead for them, Clarity, and further Acceptance of their ongoing Journey, and with this comes an increased Energy and Focus towards their Soul Contract and in particular what lies within the next Soul Contract Phases for them. At the early stages after Transitioning, the Non Physical Human can stutter through Life a little as everything seems so new and it can Take Time for them to Remember so much of what they Learned as a Non Physical Human before they Transformed to a Physical Human.

. . .

Often they still Hold Energy from their recent Physical Human Life in their Perspective Consciousness and so it's really Important for the Higher Self of the newly Transitioned Non Physical Human to Start to Trigger a new Sense of direction and Hope as well as Trigger in them Feelings of Energetic Prowess that Excites and Inspires. Encouraging them to Feel the Spiritual Term 'Can You Hear The Love' Helps to bring through what is Important to that newly Transitioned Non Physical Human Soul. It could Be a new Sense of Family and therefore the Desire to Start evolving and Creating new Non Physical relationships, or to Discover the answers to some of the questions that they had when they were a Physical Human about what Life is really like after Death, or perhaps it could Be a strong Alignment to Energy and Energy Wielding if they were a Highly Evolved Physical Human that had already honed their Energetic skills and Energetic Prowess in their Physical Life Working with Non Physical whilst Physical. Whatever it is, the Higher Self will spend a lot of Time with the newly Transitioned Soul to point them in the right direction and get them into a Place of further Allowing over what they have recently found Full Acceptance over, namely the fact that they have Transitioned and that their Life Now needs to Move on, Eternally.

This can Be quite a Realisation and often Leads the newly Transitioned Soul to Agitate negatively a little when the sheer enormity of what lies ahead Starts to Be Felt. Of course what lies ahead is a Life of Wonder and Expansion, but without Feeling Fully at Ease in your new Surroundings it's very easy to Agitate Fear for the newly Transitioned Non Physical Human. It's in these early Phases of Transition that the Non Physical Human most strongly Connects with the Spiritual Term Can You Hear The Love. It's like a song that constantly plays over and over in your Head, the Non Physical Human Feels The Soul Lovingly Agitate Continuously with the Triggers of 'Can you Hear The Love'. However unlike that song that Goes round and round in your Head, 'Can You Hear The Love' has an ever increasing positive effect on The Soul Energy, and the newly Transitioned Non Physical Human over Time is Lead to a Strengthening Understanding of their own Destiny and with this comes the Desire to Understand more and a slow return back to their Truth. Their Truth that Connects them fully back to Self Love and God's Destiny, and with this comes a Soul Swell that brings Feelings of Ethereal Knowing for All That They Are in The Ethereal Realm.

Like a seed that's laid dormant for many years suddenly Being blown to a Place where it can Start to Grow, or a distant horizon becoming Clear as it draws nearer, the newly Transitioned Non Physical Human will Feel the effects of Can You Hear The Love bringing them closer to wanting to Belong, to Create and Co-Create in this new Phase of their Life and with this comes the Energetic Shift towards Feelings of the Truth within themselves and hence of positive Influence for themselves and others.

At this point the Higher Self for that Non Physical Human will begin the process of new Introductions, Energetic Learning and the gradual Moving away of them Being Engaged in every part of every moment for the newly Transitioned Non Physical Human. For as a Physical Human their Higher Self was Aligning to, and supporting almost every part of their Life, an Energetic Under-taking of huge proportions, but not something that can Continue Eternally considering they have other Humans to Physically Incar-nate as well as other Energetic activities in Non Physical ongoing. So once the newly Transitioned Non Physical Human is at this deeper Place of Understanding the Higher Self Moves away from the more direct access and involvement of their Life Flow Path, except for the key moments in their Soul Contract Phases. Even

Pre-manifested Events in the newly Transitioned Non Physical Human's Soul Contract at this point may Now Be more Influenced by a Non Physical Guide rather than their Higher Self, although their Higher Self will always Be Notified Energetically of any specific moments of Importance.

Why 'Hear' And Not 'Feel'?

The question as to why the Spiritual Term is Can You 'Hear' The Love is Important. Whilst this Spiritual Term is ultimately Felt by the Non Physical Human, the Reference to 'Hearing' links to the Non Physical Human Connecting Unconsciously to the Thoughts of those that Love them in Non Physical that they 'Hear'. Words such as "it's so Lovely to have him back" or "I'm so Excited to Work with her on...", that could Be part of Conscious Thought from two other Non Physical Humans that are closely acquainted with the newly Transitioned Non Physical Human. This will Be Heard via the XFlow Function of the newly Transitioned Non Physical Human which is specifically Tuned at this early Transition Stage to the Spiritual Term 'Can You Hear The Love'. Perhaps they will Hear a more direct statement made to them from an old friend in Non Physical such as "hurry up we Need you to Work with us on...". These example Conscious Thoughts of others in Non Physical we have provided, the newly Transitioned Non Physical Human 'Hears' as part of the Spiritual Term 'Can You Hear The Love'. This Hearing then Triggers a subsequent Vibration of Love in them and hence further supporting them in their return to The Ethereal Realm.

Not everything that is Felt from this Spiritual Term are the Thoughts of others in Non Physical. There are other Influences that make the Non Physical Human 'Hear'. Words such as "keep Going", "you are Doing Amazingly" and "you are exactly where you are supposed to Be" are commonly Heard by the newly Transitioned Non Physical Human via 'The Truth Of You' within their Soul, and again when these are Heard they Trigger a positive Vibration in them which is Felt. The newly Transitioned Non Physical Human will also Hear 'References' from God's Destiny which Relate specifically to conversations that they previously will have had with God when Creating their own Soul Contract. A sentence such as "Remember how much you wanted to Go to Mars with me to Learn how to Use Black Holes" could specifically link to a Request that the newly Transitioned Non Physical Human made in order to Discover other Universes and other Physical Humans and Non Physical Humans. In 'Hearing' in this way from God's Destiny References, the newly Transitioned Non Physical Human Remembers, and subsequently Feels something, in this example most probably Joy, Intrigue, Belief, Hope and Desire at the thought of undertaking such an activity with God.

The Importance of Can You Hear The Love cannot Be underestimated with regards to the integration of newly Transitioned Non Physical Humans after The Full Acceptance Process and their ongoing Future as an Eternal Non Physical Being. This Spiritual Term can Do so much to Assist in new Creation and Co-Creation activities for the newly Transitioned Non Physical Human and Set them on their Path to a new Phase in their Eternal Life, full of Connection and with a momentum that Leads to a Life full of Self Love and a Life of Alignment to their Destiny and God's Destiny.

17

CONTINUING YOUR ETERNAL LIFE

Time Spent With Your Higher Self

After an Epic Physical Human Life Experience, no matter what Epic Means to you right Now, Know that for those who Transition, it was Energetically Epic what was accomplished during their Physical Life. There is no greater Impact of that Epic Energetic Influence than that of the Higher Self of the Transitioned Soul. For each Higher Self, when their Incarnation Completes Transition, wishes to spend Time with them. This is always met with such Love and Hope and Excitement as the Possibility of Being together, for Now that the Transitioned Non Physical Human Remembers in Full, it is a Wondrous Opportunity for them both and a Time for Reflection and Celebration.

There is Time spent on Reflection, which is an Opportunity to Understand in more detail around the Energetic Influences Experienced between the Higher Self and the newly Transitioned Soul during their Physical Life Experiences. It is in this Reflection

Period that so much is Understood around Soul Energy Expansion, what has been Enabled therefore and how that has Created Positive Change in The Soul Energy of the Higher Self. This is a special point in this Time of Sharing as for the newly Transitioned Soul, this is Going to bring so much Wonder and Alignment to their Purpose and Meaning. The Reason for their Physical Human Experiences and Now Fully Understanding the Influence that this has had Energetically on their Higher Self is such a positive, Soul Expanding moment. The Pride that a Higher Self has for their Incarnation is Immense and this Sharing of what their Energetic Epicness has Created for the Higher Self is an Honour for the Higher Self to explain and such a special Time that is Loved by All.

The Higher Self will Help the Transitioned Soul to Understand more detail around their Energetic Capabilities and also what Abilities remain to Be Opened and progressed as a next Phase of activity in their Eternal Life.

There is Opportunity to discuss Energetic Aspirations, for after Transition, the Non Physical Human will have Discovered so much through the Transition Process about what their Soul was able to Do, which they weren't able to Enact during their Physical Experience. So too, they will Understand what Capabilities had been Enacted yet the full extent of their 'Use' was unknown to them as a Physical Human but Now is True and Felt and Ready to Be Used.

This discussion is a Wondrous one as the Capability to Create and Expand is Immediately accessible to the newly Transitioned Non Physical Human and the Higher Self will support and Guide them on how to best Exercise and Use what they Now Understand to Be within them but will also Help them to Feel the expansive Possibilities for what happens next.

Equally, there is Time for Celebration, for the Knowing that is Shared and the incredible impact of the newly Transitioned Soul's Physical Life is discussed and Cherished and passionately Understood by the two Souls together. In this Celebration, there may Be specific Soul Aspects within the Higher Self that have been Enacted because of the newly Transitioned Non Physical Human's Physical Life Achievements, and this is also Shared between them. The Higher Self may in fact Be able to Ascend Dimensionally because of their Physical Life Achievements, which Opens up so much further Opportunity and Capability for them Energetically together. This is the most Wondrous Time of Celebration and Vibrational Enjoyment that is triumphantly Appreciated by the Higher Self.

Wanting To Say Hello

For every newly Transitioned Non Physical Human, they want to Understand how the Physical Humans in their Soul Group are getting on and also Understand if anyone is Ready to Connect with them. This sounds functional, but it is through complete Love that this willingness to Understand more comes from, yet it is not a 'yearning'. The Higher Self will often make a point of Clarity to Help determine that this isn't an essential part of Non Physical Life, yet of course all who have Transitioned want to participate and Energetically support those that they have 'left behind' in The Physical Realm. Now that they Know what they Know so well, it is with such Anticipation and Hope for a Sharing of Love that the Transitioned Non Physical Human wishes to Be Available should any Physical Human that is within their Soul Group Be Ready.

. . .

For a newly Transitioned Non Physical Human, this Energetic Presence with The Physical Realm can Be very challenging but so worth it. For they are able to Be Ubiquitous, Meaning they will Be within their Energetic Holding in the Chamber Of God and yet they will also Be Capable of Energetically Being Present with Physical Humans. Not up in the sky or in and around the Universe somewhere, but right there in the room with them. To begin with, this is in part Remembering Ubiquity, for it is something that all Created Souls before their Physical Incarnation are Capable of. By Remembering 'how' they can Be Ubiquitous, they of course want to Go and Enact it. When a newly Transitioned Soul is embarking on this Ubiquity for a 'visit' to their Physical friends, Family and Loved Ones, it is with a revived Energy, more potent than they have Experienced before they were Physical and one that has a greater Energetic Influence on them too. For this Ubiquity can Be so Powerful, so useful and so Needed by those Loved Ones in The Physical Realm and that Energy is Felt and Used by the newly Transitioned Soul that is Engaging in Ubiquity.

So, not only is there the willingness for the newly Transitioned Soul to Use their Ubiquity for this Wondrous Purpose, they may in fact Be 'Called'. This is the Energetic Reference for a Physical Human who is Asking for Connection to a Non Physical Energy, even if somewhat Unconsciously. Being 'Called' Creates an Energetic Ask between the Physical Human and the Transitioned Soul which can Be fulfilled by the newly Transitioned Soul as Soon as they are Energetically Capable. That may Be immediately after Transition Complete in some cases.

What is Magical Now to Connect to is that as part of the Acceptance Process, which has been Remembered and also Discovered by the Transitioned Non Physical Human, is that those Loved

Ones, those in their Soul Group all have Purpose, Meaning and therefore a Reason for Being. It is Understood by the Transitioned Non Physical Human about The Soul Energy of Loved ones, what they are Truly Capable of and what they were Created for including special Aspects of their Soul Energy and Important Phases of their Soul Contract. This Remembering can Be such a revelation for the Transitioning Soul as there may have been many Times and moments where in their Physical Experience, they have 'Known' that their Loved one had so much more within them but they perhaps couldn't put their finger on it. Now they can! Or perhaps they had Seen their Loved One battle and suffer through their Physical Experiences and can Understand what has Now been Energetically Enabled within them. Now, they not only Understand this but due to the Possibility of Connection, they are Capable of Helping the Physical Human that they Care so much about to Understand this too, if the Physical Human is willing, able and Capable. Willing to Connect, able to Allow and Capable to Interact.

All Non Physical Humans are bound by Energetic Law and part of that Law is about Free Will. This Means that even though the newly Transitioned Physical Human Now has all of this Insight and Understanding about their Loved ones, they are not able to intervene and Create that Understanding for them directly. For it is their Loved one's Journey in The Physical Realm, and that Must Be respected fully and any Realisation, Insight or Enacting of their Soul Contract in terms of Interaction with Non Physical Must firstly come from the Intentions of the Physical Human. It will not Be Forced, it Must Be Allowed. It Must Be chosen by that Soul living that Physical Life and never by another.

· · ·

Know that each newly Transitioned Non Physical Human Knows this and doesn't Need to 'Learn on the job'. They may Find flexible ways to Try and communicate and Guide those they Love still in The Physical Realm in any way that they can, whilst still Being bound by Energetic Law, and there are so many and varied ways that this is Possible to Do and so many newly Transitioned Souls can Be Creative with this! It is also Energetic Soul Energy Exercising for them to Try, so they really Do want to because ultimately it Helps them excel and Move quickly through Energetic Phases of their Eternal Life.

There are Chapters within this book that explain how to Connect to a Transitioned Loved One for those who wish to Allow this type of Connection and want to Understand how to Go about it Consciously.

A New Purpose

The next Phase of the Eternal Life for a newly Transitioned Soul is not to rush into what happens next but to Be Allowed to evolve to it. This is for specific Reason, for in The Ethereal Realm, there is also 'Free Will'. Some newly Transitioned Souls will wish to spend more Energy and therefore Time with their Loved Ones in The Physical Realm in the Hope they will Feel them and or wish to Connect with them. Some wish to spend their Time with those that they are reunited with in The Ethereal Realm, including Loved Ones or those from their Soul Group or their Non Physical Team members who they may have Interacted with during their Physical Life, or perhaps that they didn't Know Existed before they had Transitioned. Some wish to Settle and Enjoy Finding their 'Energetic legs' as they reDiscover Ubiquity and what that can Now Mean for them. Some Feel Certainty and Connection to an extended Reason and they will wish to Exercise and Understand more around their Capabilities in order to Achieve so much more, and some wish just to Travel and Be. How wonderful this Time is.

There are many other differing examples of what happens next in The Eternal Life, but what is a wonderful thing to Align to is the Understanding that a new Soul Contract set of Phases are Created. In this new Creation, it is the Non Physical Soul with God and the Higher Self that are the key Contributors and that Enjoy the discussion over the positive Possibilities of the new Soul Contract Phases looking forward. There will always Be a Thread of what has come before, so some of the Important Requests of the previous Soul Contract Phases that perhaps were not able to Be fulfilled whilst the Non Physical Human was in The Physical Realm, yet are still very needed, will Be discussed and a 'New Way' to Create the Possibilities of Achievement will Be included. A 'New Way' is a Spiritual Term which provides the Open ended avenue for always Finding a solution, an alternative direction, a fresh Perspective or Energetic Possibility to Enable that which is Being Focussed upon.

This is an Exciting Time for All that are involved, for there is nothing like Creation and Co-Creation, there is nothing like Collating Possibility and Potential and Opportunity and plotting a path to it with the infinite Capability available to Do so, and for there to Be Choices and actions and Selection and Interactions all along the way which Mean it isn't guaranteed to Be "exactly like this" and "exactly like that" but with High aspirations that they could Be "exactly like this" and "exactly like that". As there is no End to Eternal Life, these specific Soul Contract Phases cannot last an Eternity, there will always Be new Opportunities to Be explored and hence new Phases to Be added. The Soul Contract is frequently updated as 'Key Soul Contract Milestones' are reached or new ones Asked for, and this brings another Meeting and Agreement and Focus with God and their Higher Self to amend and to Enable the Continued evolution and Growth of the Non Physical Human and their Soul.

Opportunities

Feel into it Now, what the incredible Opportunities that Being a Physical Human Represents in The Physical Realm. There is an almost indefinite number of Possibilities for Change, for Growth, for Adaptation, for Learning, for action, for Discovery, for Choice, for Involvement, for evolvement, for Design, for Innovation, for Creation and so much more! Then Expand this Exponentially, stratospherically and Now you can Start to Sense the magnitude of Possibilities for a Non Physical Human. For there is Limitless and Endless Possibility for them. Whether it Be a specialist Focus on a particular series of Cooperative Capabilities with one specific Aspect of Energy, such as Colour or Light or Sound, and whether that Be something that is then Used or Taught or Wielded or Ignited or Co-Created with. Whether it Be a Collective engagement in Matter Creation. Whether it Be an incredible Leading Edge Guide for a Physical Human. Whether it Be a new Vision for Soul Contracts that can Energetically Create newness or modification or Insight to Help those before they Transform to a Physical Life. Whether it Be the new Influence on Nature and therefore Nature Objects on Earth or another planet. Whether it Be an Aptitude and Capability for Memory and therefore a new Configuration or Adaptation can Be made for an Influence on a Soul Model or the Physical Human Body Design. Whether it Be a Focus simply and Purely on one particular Universal Law and the new Engagement Opportunities or Facets or Enactments that it can provide. Whether it Be a Desire to Understand and Learn and Grow through Interaction and Experiences with other Non Physical

Souls. Whether it Be pushing the current limits of Energetic Travel and Disbursement in Ubiquity to Find a New Way.

Limitless, Endless, Possibility.

So, with the Concepts that have been spoken of and with the Energy of Creation and Cooperation and Collective and Singular Influence, there is SO much that can Be Eternally Enjoyed and Flowed to and evolved through and Experienced. What we have stated here has only scratched the surface of what a Non Physical Human can Do. As each Non Physical Human is 'Love Labelled' and full of Energy, this isn't to Be mistaken for an exhausting Eternal Life. It is fulfilling. There is newness. There is Wonder and Magic and Excitement and Progress and Change and Love. So, so much Love. Love in such Abundance it would Be impossible to fathom. So think of a moment in your Life where you Felt so Full of Love that you almost Felt like you would explode and implode at the same Time. It is like that. And an endless Energy of it and the Capability to Feel Balanced with it, so it isn't ever too much. Just the Capability to increase it on demand, and the Flow of Powerful Love. The Capability to Soothe it down and make it that Gentle kind of quieter safe Love that just Feels nourishing and Giving and Pure. This kind of Love Creates Momentum and willingness to Be. Be All That You Are.

This is why we say, when you are Living this Physical Life, to 'Choose Love'. For Love is beyond. Beyond what we have comprehended it to Be. It is the fabric of The Soul Energy for all Humans. It is accessible by all Physical Humans and all Non Physical Humans. It is in the Creation of all things. It Gives. It Flows and Allows you to Flow. By Choosing Love, you are Energetically

Allowing yourself to Be so much more of All That You Are as you are Living this Physical Life or Non Physical Life. The more you are You in your Physical Life, the more Opportunity you have in your Eternal Non Physical Life. Yet, if you can't, if you can't Find your way to it as a Physical Human, either Now, or later, or Soon, Know that you will. For this Love and this Opportunity awaits you when you Transition. But please we Ask that you Try to Live this Now, for you don't have to wait until you Transition to Experience the greatest of Love.

IV

UNDERSTANDING GRIEF AND CONNECTION TO TRANSITIONED LOVED ONES

18

FOR THOSE WHO ARE STILL ASKING "WHY DID YOU LEAVE ME?"

The Physical Human Experience can Be so Challenging. Yes, of course there is all the Possibility of Wonder along your Journey, yet there are Times, and the loss of a Loved One can Be one of those Times, where Being a Physical Human and Feeling all the Feelings is just hard.

Even in the Recognition of this book, the Insight and the Understanding that it Creates for you as you read it, for many, it will Be Soothing to Know and Connect to, yet it will not Take away that gnawing of Grief, Sadness or Devastation that is still Present. Being able to Know and Feel the Truth that your Loved One is Eternal, that confirmation of what you either already Felt to Be True or Hoped to Be True Now 'Is'. Yet, the Physical yearning for that person to Be in the room with you, to have a hug from them, the missing of their face in the crowd on special occasions, that simple Hearing the Sound of their voice or Hearing their laugh or wanting to Hear their opinion on something that is Important to you; it is enough to break a dam of Emotion so Powerful within you that you Fear you wouldn't Survive the flood.

That yearning is great, sizeable and flares up. When your Loved One first Transitions, this yearning is Strong but it Does also Grow and it Grows because the aftermath of the loss and all the things that Take Place straight afterwards, Create different Emotions for so many. It is once the weeks Start to Move by and Life is Continuing to Be Lived by those that are left behind that the True Grief can commence.

True Grief can come in Waves. One moment you can Connect to the Truth and Feeling of Eternalness and with that, comes relief and some Ease, yet all of a sudden, a song that gets played or an event that gets planned, and along comes the Wave of Grief that you thought you were Holding back and Doing ok with. When it comes, it Feels like a tidal Wave and often you Try to suppress it, Control it, Revoke it, ride it, climb it, or just let it Take you where it wants to Go.

It would Be remiss of us to suggest you should not Feel this way, simply because you Know what you Now Know. What we Hope to Help you with however is a smoother ride along those Waves. That when they surface, they don't Pull you into a Continuous riptide of Grief that ultimately Changes you, that Holds you back, that indeed Stops you from Living and Creating and Being. That you Recognise that Wave for what it is. A moment in Time. That as quick as it came, it can also Go. That calm seas are Possible. That Waves can Create Momentum. Momentum for Change in a new direction.

· · ·

One of the reasons for Grief to Be so prominent and the Continued raging sea full of these Waves is in the Asking of "Why?".

Why did you have to Go?

Why did you Leave me?

Why couldn't you Be saved?

Why Now?

Why couldn't it have been later?

Why couldn't you have Lived?

Why couldn't have something else happened instead?

Why you?

Why did this Manifest?

Why were you Taken from me?

Why didn't you Stop it?

Why didn't you Try?

Why didn't you choose differently?

Why did you choose this Soul Contract?

Why did I choose this Soul Contract?

Why didn't you look after yourself?

Why wasn't there a cure?

Why couldn't we have just one more day?

Why didn't you Hold on?

Why God, Why?

In the Searching for the answers to the 'Why', the Grief turns from small undulating series of breakers on the shore to a cacophony of crashing thunderous stormy Waves. The water can deepen and Take you further out to sea. So too the Grief. You can Start to question the fabric of what you Truly Believe and Understand to Be True. Yet, it doesn't have to Be this way.

Can every question of 'Why' have an answer? Yes. Will it Be the answer you want to Hear? That depends. It depends on whether you are actually Asking and expecting an Answer. It depends on whether you are Asking in order to Understand and to Let Go and you are Ready to Hear or Feel the True answer, or whether in fact you are Asking because you are only wanting to Hear that in fact something different has Taken Place and the person that you Love has in fact not Transitioned at all. Or that there is a very special and Unique thing that happened to that Loved One outside of all we have Shared with you so far.

It can also depend on who it is that you are Asking and whether you are Allowing the answer to Flow to you. If it is another Physical Human, they will answer most often based on their Perspective and you may not Feel the Truth of their answer. If you are Asking God, your Higher Self, the Transitioned Loved One or another Non Physical Human, you will always get the answer but it may not yet Be in the way that you Understand how to Hear it or Feel it.

.   .   .

For the Truth in any answer Must Be Felt by you. In Asking "why?", often you are not Allowing the Truth of what has happened and often, not Allowing the answer, and in Doing so, you are in fact Creating the stormy sea. In the Feeling of the Truth, that your Loved One is still accessible, still available to you, just in a different Form, some of the 'whys' Start to Go. Stating these Truths below will Help you to Start to answer your whys.

The Truth is it was the Right Time

The Truth is it was their Journey not mine

The Truth is that I can't Change this Outcome. The Truth Is that my Loved One can't either

The Truth is that we are Eternal

The Truth is that my Loved One matters and so too Do I

The Truth is that there is only Love where my Loved One Now is

The Truth is that I am able to Connect with my Loved One, in fact they are with me right Now

The Truth is that they are only a Feeling away

The Truth is that their Life mattered

The Truth is that they are evolving in their Eternal Life and I can evolve too, both Now whilst I am Physical and later, when I am Non Physical

The Truth is that I really don't want to Feel this terrible

The Truth is that there is no expected duration of Grief that I Need to fulfil

The Truth is I can Feel what I Feel, that nobody can Stop me

The Truth is that my Loved One wants me to Move forward as quickly as I can to Start Truly Living, Creating and Feeling good again as soon as possible

The Truth is that I cannot Go back in Time to Change 'What Was'

The Truth is that I can Energetically remember Experiences with my Loved One and I can Focus on the good Feelings and remembering for it will have more value to me

The Truth is that I can Let Go, I don't Need to Hold onto Grief

The Truth is I don't Need to Be Sad nor am I expected to Be Sad by my Loved One that has Transitioned

The Truth is the sooner I can Let Go, the sooner I can Accept with Truth my Loved One is Eternal and has Transitioned, the sooner I can Connect with them again

The Truth is I am not Being punished

The Truth is I am not Being Targeted by bad luck or any other negative Influence

There are so many Truths that you could Feel. Truths that would really break up that Swell, that would calm that sea of Grief. From this Place, you Feel more moments of Calm, more moments of You-ness. Some Hope. Some Love for you. Some Love for them. Some Peace, a stillness within you that you Feel the Truth that it is Going to Be ok, that Life will Continue for you and you will Find a way. We recommend always, that you Allow yourself to Focus upon You. That you Tend to your own Emotional Truths and Notice how you Feel and Act on it, by navigating through it, by Being Honest with yourself first and foremost and Connecting into you.

. . .

We Know however during a Time of loss, that it is difficult when in the navigation of your own Emotions relating to loss, that you must Interact with other Physical Humans. So often, if left to your own devices and in many cases, you would in fact Be able to navigate these tricky waters, to ride the surf, to Take your Time to Learn how and Understand and Let Go. Yet, in the constant reminders from others or for their Needing support or Help or your Guidance in Helping them to navigate through their Grief, you are often drawn back in and having to Go over and over the very thing that you have been Trying to Move on from.

It is simple, but not easy, to Focus only upon yourself in these moments.

Feel Compassion yes, of course, but Notice when others' Emotions are Triggering your own Low Vibration and Starting to Swell that sea and when you Notice, immediately Take Action. That action could Be to as quickly as you can, exit the conversation so you can reBalance. That action could Be Aligning to a Truth you have already Created. That action could Be Asking the other person who is Needing your involvement in their Experience of Grief whether they are willing to Change their Perspective, whether they are willing to Allow, whether they are Ready to Let Go just a little.

By involving yourself in others' Experiences of Grief, not only can it exacerbate your own and Stop you from Allowing the Truths you have already Created by not Living them, you are also Enabling the Prolonged Energy of Grief for the person that is Needing to Share it with you. For they are Responsible for how they Feel. They cannot Create a Low Vibrational Emotion within you, only you can Do that. So too conversely, you cannot Create a High Vibrational Emotion within them just because you Feel Aligned to a Broader Perspective. You are however able to Influence each other, but only in whatever way you Allow it to Be so.

For if you are able to Take Action, such as one described above, you are limiting the negative Influence of another on you and increasing the positive Influence on them. If you don't Notice how it is making you Feel and you Continue for long enough, you will Allow the negative Influence of another to Be predominant and in Doing so, your positive Influence will Be difficult to bring forth.

"What About Being There For Grieving Children?"

Surely we adults, are Responsible for Helping children navigate through Grief and we Need to Be there for them? The answer is, of course yes. But your Responsibility is also to Allow the Responsibility to Be theirs, and this can Be Done by not telling them how they are to Feel or telling them how they Do Feel Now. By Showing a child that you are a safe Place to come, that you will Help them of course, but that you won't tell them how they Need to Feel. That you will Help them to Understand these Feelings, for often children Feel so much and yet can't quite articulate the Feelings. Explaining that it may Be difficult for you to talk about, but those are your Feelings, not their Feelings. You don't need to fix a child who is suffering from Grief, for you cannot, but you can Help them Understand in the same way that we have Shared with you, that they have the Opportunity to navigate these Emotions. By Understanding that the same True Grief Waves will Be Present for them too and when, or if they come, that they will Know what to Do. That they simply Need to tell you a Wave has come, and you will Know what to Do to Help them.

. . .

Yet you can only Do this if you are practicing this yourself.

The shock of the loss is very Present in and around the Time of the Death itself. If a child is Truly Allowed to Feel, their Emotions will Feel very big and often will Be very visible. In these big Emotions, some Powerful things are occurring. They are learning and Understanding so much about Love, about Life, about Feeling. Children will Seek to Understand about 'what happens when you Die', because they have an inherent Soul Knowing of it, so they may Ask. If the key concepts of this book are Shared with them, very quickly they will Feel the Truth of it and that Tidal Wave we speak of will Dissipate. For children are so Open to the Truth, to Feeling it. If they don't in the moment, that is ok, for sometimes when such powerful Emotions in a combination such as Grief are Taking Place, it can Be hard to Settle on the Truth. Sometimes too, a child will pick up on whether you Believe it to Be True and if not, they will Sense that and therefore may Deny your words.

If you speak to a child who has recently Experienced the loss of a Loved One, and they Connect to the fact their Energy is Eternal, that they are with them, that they can speak with them whenever they want to and they might Hear their voice or Feel their Love, it can Create a ripple of Change within that child that Moves them from Being ensconced in Fear about Death to a deeper, long lasting Understanding that although no longer Physically here, that Loved One is still very Present, whenever they Need them. This Creates an Environment for a child to then Continue to Ask whenever they Need to, to Continue to Notice when they are Feeling a Wave of Emotion and to either Learn to navigate it themselves or indeed come to you for support.

. . .

It Opens the door for them to Feel the Energy of their Loved One. To Take that as far as they wish. This too must Be something that is Allowed by the Adults in the child's vicinity, for it is often the Adults that Fear what children speak of in relation to Connection to Non Physical yet so often, children Do it so naturally and openly and it is so easy for them to Do it. So, if this is something that you Feel Good to talk about with that child that has come to you and if they are receptive and Allowing and Feel Good about it, let them Continue to talk to you about it. You never Know what they can in turn teach you about the very same subject.

Knowing what you Now Know, because of what you have read and how you have Felt the Truth of it, Allow it. Allow it in all Forms, no matter what that Takes. Allow yourself to Flow with it too, in this Allowing. Try not to Force it, whether that Be a conversation with another Adult, child or otherwise. Whether that Be Trying to Connect to your Loved One, Trying to Create a Truth which you just can't Feel yet, or Trying to Get Over It. By Flowing to it, it will Feel easier. By Forcing it, you just Create Resistance, both for you and potentially for others. So Be Easy on yourself, as often as you can. Allow as often as you can. Flow as often as you can.

"What About The Loss Of A Child, Surely That Is The Hardest To Feel The Truth Of?"

"Emotions Don't Care About Experiences".

This was first written in 5th Dimension Earth's book Believe. Of course, for anyone who has had a child that they Love so dearly, in particular, a child that is part of them in this Physical Life, for us to say these words to you, you may want to throw this book against the wall. Yet, it is the same Experience. The same loss, the Waves of Grief, the coming to terms with the Emotions, the Letting Go of the Physical, the Moving away from the yearning for them to Be back with you; therefore we offer the same Truths as mentioned earlier in this chapter. It is the same Transition Process for that little one, or even not so little one, for regardless of age, a child to you is still your child, no matter how old. It is the same 'whys' that have been mentioned at the Start of this Chapter. It is therefore the same Guidance that Follows.

Yet, in this similarity, there is a little more that we wish to Share with you. For the great Grief and burden of the Knowing a child that has Transitioned for any remaining living Parent, is the Fear and lack of Understanding about what happens to them. Even Being able to relate to the Transition Process and completely Understanding it, to Know that their Soul is indeed Eternal and therefore they will Go on to Live, to flourish, to Grow and to Evolve in their Wondrous Energy that you Knew whilst they were Physical, there is still the question around who is looking after them. For you Know their Energy to Be the age at which they Transitioned. Yet, Now you Understand that their Soul will have been much older, for their Soul's Eternal Life commenced when they were Created. No matter their age at Transition, whether it Be a mere few hours of Physical Life or indeed Precious years of Physical Experience, their Soul was already evolved and so with it, came some Understanding of a potentially shorter Physical Life. In this unfolding Understanding, you can Connect to the painful part, that they are no longer Existing within their Physical Body but they are Free and you are able to Connect with them still, to Love them still, to Know them still, to Understand them still and also how their Soul is evolving, and therefore what they are able to Share with you becomes an evolved conversation. For as Time Goes on, so too Does their Non Physical Soul evolvement. They will still Be them. They will still bear their Physical Human name, their Energy, the Feeling of them is still True. Yet just as if they were Physical, they are Growing and Wondering, Creating and Connecting, Meeting and Participating and Living. Their Higher Self is with them always, they are never alone. Any Transitioned Loved One from your Family is also with them. They will also have many other incredible Non Physical Human friends that are with them, Expanding them and Showing them how to evolve, as well as them Expanding and evolving others.

Even in these words, you may Feel some temporary solace, yet we Understand the pain may still Be there and that you may not Feel Ready for any of this information. One day you just might. Perhaps today, this seed of Hope for an evolved relationship with your Transitioned child can Be planted and over Time, and as you navigate your way through how you Feel, you can come to a Place of Growth within your own Soul and an Energy of willingness to Try. There is no Force here from us to you, only Love and True Compassion for all you have endured through this Experience. Trust that with Hope you will one day Feel Ready, your child will Be there for you whenever you are.

"But My Baby Didn't Even Get To Live, What Happened To Them?"

A 'lost' baby is a phrase so often Used, yet they are never lost, this we promise you. For any baby that was Created, no matter under which circumstances your baby was lost, even though your baby that wasn't able to become Fully Physical and Commence their Physical Life Experiences, they were Created for a Purpose. That Purpose was to become a new Higher Self.

· · ·

There is a specific Chapter in 5th Dimension Earth's book Believe which details this Understanding more. Please Know that your baby's Precious Life mattered and Goes on to matter so much Now in The Ethereal Realm. Know that it was meant to Be, that their Soul was Created so that they become a Higher Self, and that this could indeed have Been Premanifested, you couldn't have Changed it no matter what you did.

For many who chose to terminate a pregnancy, Know that this Experience was also Premanifested and that The Soul that you Created was always Destined to Be a Non Physical Higher Self. Know that your role in this is Precious for it Takes God and also the Energy of two Physical Humans in order to Now Manifest the Creation of a Higher Self. Originally only God's Energy was Needed to Create Higher Self Souls on his own. Yet Now it is God and the Physical Human Energy that Enables this Wondrous Non Physical Entity to Be Formed and it is the Energy of the Physical Humans that Helps to bring such greater Possibility for the new Higher Self that is Created, and so Take comfort that although baby of yours that didn't Live a Physical Life they will instead Live a Wondrous Non Physical Life because of you. The Premanifestation of this Higher Self Creation Forms part of the two Physical Humans' Soul Contracts, it is therefore something that you would have agreed to in The Ethereal Realm before your own Physical Life, and this would have been something that will have provided you with such Pride because you would have been Responsible in part for the Creation of a new Higher Self.

Allow the Magic and Wonder of this if you can. Allow the Hope of this if you can and if you are not Ready to just yet, that is completely Understood. If and when you are ever Ready to, you are able to Connect with that precious Soul that you Created in the same way we describe that of a child that has Transitioned. In particular, in the Knowing that they are indeed a Higher Self, there is so much to Understand about their Energy and what they are Capable of and why they were Created. You are able to get to Know them and also, get to Find out how they evolve as they Grow Energetically and become Capable, incredible, awesome Higher Selves Ready to Incarnate Physical Human Souls themselves.

Grief and The 'Believe Releasing Process'

For those of you that have read 5th Dimension Earth's book Believe you will Understand that the key Understanding within it is of the Higher Self and how Connecting with them can Lead you to Emotional Freedom through the Letting Go of the past in a way that Truly Stops you from Generating Low Vibration from 'any' past Experience. The book also Shows how to Connect to Love, and stay there. This is Done by Working with your Higher Self to reConnect you to key past Experiences and for your Higher Self to bring forward a new 'Love Labelled' Perspective of that past Experience in order to 'Relabel' your Subconscious Mind Memories that you Trigger by the second. A Subconscious Mind Memory that is Love Labelled Generates High Vibration, but of course the opposite is True for Fear Labelled Subconscious Mind Memories which can fill your Physical Body with Low Vibration Continuously.

The Believe Releasing Process sensitively and over Time Follows this principle and Allows you to Let Go the 'Fear' Attached to many of those past Experiences, some of which may Be Locked or Hidden and therefore still not remembered or fully remembered, but still Triggering Low Vibration in you. Your Higher Self brings you to new Understanding about negative past Experiences to

Help Clarify why things happened and Help you to Connect to Love for those Experiences as well as your Journey and also the Journey of others, in that order. The Believe Releasing Process brings so much Self Love, Hope and Wonder back into your Life as you Lead yourself to a more permanent Love Labelled Existence. So many have Followed this Wondrous God Given process and today are Now Living the fullest of Lives, Expanding Energetically, Loving Fully, and Connecting to 'All That They Are'.

We speak of this to acknowledge that Grief is hard to overcome. We have provided some Loving Guidance in this book to Help you to Move forward but we Understand that even in Reconnection with a Loved One that has Transitioned, it can still Be hard to overcome, for they will never Be Physical with you again. It is the Believe Releasing Process that we Encourage every one of you that is reading this book to look towards if you are struggling with your Grief over the loss of a Loved One. It really can bring you to a Place of Peace and Acceptance and Set you to a new Perspective that Allows you to Be able to look forwards and to Consider the Opportunities that can Be there for you in a new Non Physical Human relationship with a Transitioned Loved One.

19

FOR THOSE WHO ARE FEELING "I'M NOT READY TO GO"

We have spoken of Grief so far as the Emotion of those that are left behind. Yet, you may Be reading this book in the Understanding that you Know that your own Physical Human Experience is Soon to come to a conclusion. We Hope that in fact you have many, many healthy and Happy years ahead of you, but we Understand that for some the imminence of Transition is close and this Chapter is for you.

For you may well already Be Grieving. Grieving for those Future moments that you Know are no longer possible. Grieving for the missed Opportunities. Regret for the Times you said no when you really wanted to say yes. The Sense of wishing for just one more of 'this', or to Experience 'that' one last Time. We wish more than anything that the anguish you are Feeling can Be reduced by some simple words, by a technique or a promise or a fact. Try to Change your Now to a Now that you reflect on. A Now when you Enjoy every little thing, every moment of Wonder, of Life and Feeling as good as that can Be, even if it is small, just a glimpse of something good that you put your attention to and your Focus upon.

Choose the best moments of your Life. Write them down. Speak them out loud. Feel if there is something unsaid that you wish to Be said and say it. Don't Hold back on Love, any Love that you Feel. Give it All. Leave it All here. You'll have more Soon than you could ever Imagine after Transition but don't wait until then. Love BIG in as many moments as you can. Bigger than you ever have. Love someone who is Caring for you, Love anyone who is visiting or calling, Love anyone who is Loving you. Love the sky, Love the television, Love the sunrise, Love the tree you can See, Love the flowers you can smell. In this Loving, it will make YOU Feel better. You can literally fill your day with such small moments of Love that when added altogether, they become a giant day of Love! Then this giant day of Love can Lead onto another, and another. You will Find the days are longer, have more Meaning and are not awash with Despair. In these days of Love you are choosing Love again and again. You are Noticing when you are slipping into those spiralling thoughts of Doom and Sadness and you choose Love again. You say "no", this Life is for Living right Now because right Now is all that matters and in Doing so, Love comes to you.

You can choose most Importantly to Love You. Love you for All that you are, all you were too. You can choose to Accept that nothing was your Fault, for this Understanding is what is to come so why not Allow yourself that Now? Feel and Allow that Truth to Be Activated by you. The Truth that you Do not Take Blame, for things you did or didn't Do, nor for the things you did or didn't say. What you did or didn't think or act upon. None of it was or is your Fault. In this Truth, you can Align to your Physical Human

Life Journey. Your Journey that was full of Emotion, full of Fear at Times, full of Love in others. Align to the fact that you cannot Go back and rewrite the 'What Was' and because of this, you can choose instead to Let Go. You Do not Need to Ask for forgiveness for there is nothing to forgive, only to Energetically Forget, for when you Forget this comes as a Consequence of Letting Go and you will then Find Love and Freedom. So Let Go. Be Free. Free of What Was. Even if it is just for today, or tomorrow. That is enough to Feel what it Feels like to Be Free. Feel it Now, today, don't waste another moment of not Feeling Free.

In this Feeling Free, you bring yourself to some Acceptance. Acceptance of your Journey. Acceptance of your Now. Acceptance of what did Go right. Acceptance of the Hope of what awaits you. Acceptance that you are Loved Now, even if you haven't Felt it fully. Acceptance that there is Hope for what comes next. Acceptance that you Do not, and will not lose your True Energetic Identity, and therefore you will Continue to still Live. Acceptance that after you Transition you are still able to Connect, Communicate and Love your Loved Ones as they Go about their Physical Human Experience and that if they Allow it, so much more is Possible for you and them to Continue your relationship once you have gone through the Transition Process. Find Acceptance of those who you Feel pain towards right Now, due to their Disconnection, or yours. You will Feel differently towards them once you Transition and you will have a new Loving Perspective that awaits you with regards to those Physical Humans that cause you such pain Now. But why not Align to the Possibility that you can Create that Loving Perspective right Now, even if they don't.

Find Acceptance that Foregoing your Physical Body is a Change, but one that you will and can adapt to. Acceptance that your Physical Body at Times has caused you suffering and you are Ready for that Physical suffering to end. Acceptance that when it is the Right Time that you will still have the Opportunity to keep Loving and Feeling but as a Non Physical Human.

20

CONNECTING TO A TRANSITIONED LOVED ONE

There is a lot of Fear, nervousness, trepidation and Emotional risk for some relating to even attempting to Connect to a Transitioned Loved One. What If it doesn't Work? What If I can't Feel them? What If I don't like it? What If it isn't them? How will I Know it's them? So many questions that we will Try to anticipate and answer for you so that you Feel that this is something that you are wanting to Try.

For wanting to Try to Connect is the first step. If you just Know that you don't, it is Important that you listen to this Truth within and you don't attempt it, for it is highly unlikely to Work, not Impossible however, just highly unlikely. How Do you get to wanting to Try? You Need to Feel the Truth of so much of what has been Shared and Allow it to resonate with you fully. In this Truth Alignment, you will naturally Move to a Place where any Fear that you have about Failure around Connecting either Goes altogether or Dissipates enough to Allow your wanting to Try to Be the predominant Energy.

. . .

The second most Important Energy for you to Be in is Being 'Ready to Allow'. Connection is a two way process. It isn't just your Transitioned Loved One's Energy Flowing to you. You Need to Be Ready to Allow it. That Means Feeling Balanced. That Means not ramping up Fear. That Means a Knowing that you are wanting this Connection and therefore you will Consciously Allow it.

Know that your Transitioned Loved One is always wanting to Try to Connect, so they will definitely Be Doing their part. The only caveat to this is around Time and how far through the Transition Process they are. For if they are still Going through Transition, they will not Be able to Communicate with anyone who is Physical.

What is not widely Understood is that it Takes a huge amount of Energy for a Transitioned Soul to Connect to anyone still in The Physical Realm, yet always, they are wanting to Try. When a Non Physical Human has recently Transitioned, their Connection to you will Be short in the first instance, relating to the huge Energy Capacity that it Takes in order to Be Present and available to Connect with Physical Humans for them.

"What Will It Be Like To Connect With A Transitioned Loved One?"

This Experience will Be many and varied. The key things to Understand is that your Loved One will Show themselves as still them to you. This could Be Aligned to a particular point as you would remember them from their Physical Life, but they could also Show themselves to you as an older Soul, especially if it has been many years since their Physical Death. They may also Show themselves to you in a way that you would not have Seen them in their Physical Human Life and this would Be because they would Be Showing you the way they Allow Non Physical Souls to See them Now in The Ethereal Realm.

There are a couple of specific things to Understand about what happens when you Want to Try to Connect and this is about the Receiving Process. Firstly, you Hold the Energy and Intention that this is what you want to Do. Secondly, the Non Physical Soul you want to Connect to is Ready to Connect also. At this point you are Ready for an Energy Exchange.

They will Be near you and their Energy will Be Present and with you where you are Physically, you just may not Be able to See them. In order to Understand their Energy, you Translate with it. You are Translating Vibration, so their Energy is at a different Frequency and in Translating this different Frequency, you are able to Interpret it. Finally, during this Translation of Energy Process, you are then able to Receive. Receiving Means that you are able to Hold, Interpret and Understand what is Being Translated for you Vibrationally by your Transitioned Loved One. Depending on how best you are able to Translate in that moment of Trying to communicate with them (this can Change as you evolve and Do it more often) you may Feel, Hear, See or just Know that you are together.

With Feeling Translation, you will Feel their Energy Physically. You may Feel skin tingles, you may Feel Love spread through your Chest, you may Feel like their 'arm' is around your shoulders or that they are kissing you on your cheek. With Hearing, you may

Hear their voice in your Head, perhaps something that they Used to say, even a laugh or a verbal mannerism. With Seeing, you may See their Energy, you may See them almost as clearly as they are sitting right next to you. Seeing can Be Translated by you in two ways, Seeing through your eyes as if they are right there in front of you, or Seeing them behind your eyes and almost like a projection of a movie screen. With Knowing, you Cognitively Understand that they are with you. This can Be one of the hardest ways to Translate with a Non Physical Soul to Start with but a Wondrous Exchange of Knowing.

It can Take some Trust and some Time in order to Truly Believe for many that you are actually Translating and Receiving from a Loved One, but keeping it simple, Believing and persevering will quickly bring you to the Acceptance that they Truly are with you.

"What Kind Of Things Will They Say?"

Initially, it may Be just a brief sentence or you may just Feel that they are letting you Know that they Love you. When a Soul has recently Transitioned, it Takes some Time to get into the Energetic Flow of Being able to Communicate more fully with anyone in The Physical Realm. Therefore, often, if they have recently Transitioned, it may Be a sentence worth, it may just Be letting you Know that they are ok, in fact more than ok, and they can Be with you in this way whenever you are wanting to Try. Over Time as you both Tune to each other's Frequency the Translation gets easier and this is when you can expect to have some more engaging Interactions full of Love and Understanding as well as Fun and Joy.

"It Makes Me Feel Too Sad To Try"

Your Vibration is really Important when Connecting with any Non Physical Soul, and especially with your Loved One where your Emotions can Be difficult to keep Balanced. If you are Feeling full of Sadness and Despair and then you Try to Connect, those Emotional Vibrations you are Feeling clutter and cloud Energetically the very Place that you Need to have Freely Available in order to Receive. This can make Correct Translation and Receiving impossible and that then Creates more Sadness because you Feel that they have really gone and that Connecting with them isn't Possible. Yet it is. It is just you will Need to Be Vibrationally in a better Place in order to Allow that Connection.

Also, the Feeling that can Be preempted is that you will Feel worse after you have Connected because it will make you Feel the loss all over again. It is from this Place that we say to you, it isn't easy to Let Go of the loss and the Sadness, but as quickly as you can and are able, you can Continue your relationship with your Transitioned Loved One. Yes, it is different. Yes, it has Changed. But is there Possibility that it has Changed in a Wondrous way? Is it Possible that this Change could Mean incredible things for you both? Is it Possible that by Connecting with them you can Feel them and Love them and Know them still? Is it Possible that by Connecting with them you can Learn from them and you can gain some new Insight about them, perhaps about their previous Physical Life or about what they are Doing Now in The Ethereal Realm as a Non Physical Human?

Remember that you are not Being made to Do something that you just aren't Ready for, quite the opposite. The recommendation is that you only Do this when you are wanting to Try and when you are Ready to Allow. Only you will Know when this is True for you. There is no Time limit either, so Take your Time and Be Ready when you are Ready, whenever that is. Just Know that those Possibilities we speak of are waiting for you.

"Why Do I Need To Ask?"

In interacting with Non Physical in any way, there are a couple of fundamental things that will really Help you to Understand. Firstly, you Need to Set the Intention to Connect with them simply by Asking. Secondly, you need to Be Vibrationally in the right Place. Thirdly, you need to Be prepared to Ask. Ask simple, clear and easy to answer questions. It's not that they cannot Interact intelligently with you but Translation and Receiving will Be much easier to Understand for you if you keep questions short and to a specific point. Ask for contact. Ask them to Be with you. Ask to Feel them. Ask how they are right Now. Ask where they are right Now. Ask and Ask and Ask some more, but in the Asking, you Must also Allow. Allow the answer, Allow the Energy contact, Allow the Interaction, Allow the Flow of Receiving. Patience is key.

Here are some other simple questions that you will Find easy to Receive answers for. As your Receiving evolves then your general interactions and the types of questions that you Ask can also evolve.

Can you Give me a Vibrational Hug?

What is it like for you Now that you have Transitioned?

Can you Show me how I can Know it is you when you come to See me?

Can I Ask for your Help?

Can you tell me something that I Need to Know?

What Does it Feel like to Be a Non Physical Human?

Are you with friends, anyone I will Know? If so, who?

What is the best thing you have Learnt so far?

I would Love to Understand more about what I have Learnt in this book, can you teach me?

I have something that I'm struggling with, can I talk to you about it?

So often, the Focus is upon Connecting and then expecting a 'message' to come through of something that your Transitioned Loved One Needs to get to you, yet by Energetic Law, Physical Humans Must Ask. Ask questions of Non Physical Humans. In Asking questions, it Allows the Non Physical Human to answer, for otherwise it can Break the fundamental Energetic Boundary of Free Will, which they are unable to Do.

Getting really good at Asking questions is the best way to advance your Receiving with your Loved One. So often, we run out of questions and they are right here with us. Or, we just can't think of what to Ask. This can Be a great thing to pre-plan and have some questions available in order to Do this. You can See that most of the questions above are Yes/No types of questions. This is quite a good way to Start to Build your confidence and to Trust in your Receiving. Over Time, you can Go for some more open-ended questions, such as "what Does it Feel Like to Be a Non Physical Human?", or "what's Life like in other Universes?".

. . .

If you are Asking really broad questions, you can expect really broad answers, for Non Physical Humans aren't always able to Exchange with other Physical Humans in a way that Physical Humans would together because of Energetic Law. For example they could not say "you have Asked me this yet I Know you really Mean to Ask me that", they Must answer only what you have Asked. This is also why to Start with, the conversation can Feel a bit one sided (your side!) as the answers are a little short, depending on the questions you have been Asking. These broad questions and answers can Be somewhat frustrating as it Feels vague, yet your Transitioned Loved One is absolutely Capable of answering in detail and providing you with so much Insight, so just get practicing Asking questions in a way that they can answer you.

Something really helpful that everyone can Align to is to just Take the pressure off yourself. If you can get yourself into a Vibration of 'I'm just Going to See what happens' and treat any Interaction with your Transitioned Loved One like they are really here with you and not something that is scary or weird or super Important, it will really Help for any Interaction to Flow. For so often, the Importance that is Placed on this Interaction is the very thing that Stops the Flow of it and limits what can Be Experienced between you. A great Vibrational Place to Be in is that your Transitioned Loved One is getting Used to communicating with you in this way and you are getting Used to communicating with them in this way, even though you Know them so well, this type of Interaction is new and when anything is new, it can Take a little Time and a few Goes to get into the Flow.

Also, Try to Align to the fact that this isn't a one-off Experience. It isn't that you have this one Opportunity to get it right and if you don't, that's it, it can never happen again. As long as you keep Intending and wanting to Try, so too will your Transitioned Loved One, so Relax about it as much as you can and Take the pressure off yourself around the significance and Importance of it. What If it was ordinary for you that you interact with your Transitioned Loved One, on a daily or weekly basis or just whenever you wanted a catch up? What If any Time you missed them, you Asked for a hug and you got it, Vibrationally yes but you still got it. What If you could Find out so much about what they are Now evolving to in The Ethereal Realm? What If you could Ask them all about what it is like to Be in The Ethereal Realm and get the answers? What If you could chat with them as you are Going about your day, at Work or in the supermarket and you can just Feel them Being with you?

This Connection doesn't Mean that you haven't Let Go. It Means that your relationship has evolved. It Means that you Recognise that they are Truly with you still and will Be as long as you keep Intending it to Be so.

"Why Do They Come To Me In My Dreams?"

You will have Set an Intention in some way, perhaps Asked for a sign that they are with you and ok, or perhaps more Consciously tried to Connect, or just missed them so much and wished you could hug them, or maybe even been raging and Asking lots of 'whys'. Any of these scenarios is an Intention by you to Feel or Hear or have answered something by them.

When you are asleep, the normal Resistance that you have as you are Consciously Going about your day is lifted. What is Resistance? It Represents the Low Vibration that is predominantly Fear,

Fear of any kind. It could Be Fear of Failure. It could Be Fear of Loss. It could Be Sadness or Devastation or Anger. Whatever Fear is Present, as discussed earlier, this causes that Low Vibration to clutter up the space you have in order to Translate their Energy and also to Receive them. So what can lack of Resistance Enable? Translation! This is why in your sleep, when you are not Consciously activating those Fears in the moment you are able to Receive more easily from them, although because you have been asleep often the Receiving is assumed to just Be a dream. Although your dreams could Trigger Low Vibration in you, your Conscious Thought is less Active and so your Fears of Connecting with your Transitioned Loved One have a greater chance of Being avoided and with this you Generate less Low Vibration and hence have better Translation Capability. Of course if you have a Fear of Connection with Non Physical Humans, this may Mean that your dreams Start more negatively and Low Vibrational. If you end up Feeling Sadness after you wake, this is a good indication of the Emotional Activation of what it is that you have Truly been Feeling in your sleep, in particular if you are Going through Grief. When those Waves of Low Vibration hit you when you sleep and any kind of contact with your Transitioned Loved One can Be difficult to Maintain.

"I've Heard That If Someone Has Been Transitioned For A Long Time It Is Hard To Connect To Them"

Not for you. If you have visited another, perhaps a Spiritual Medium or Psychic and this has been said to you, it is because they have not been able to Translate with that Non Physical Human's Soul Energy. Yet Trust that it is always Possible for you, just Go to The Energetic Enablement Tools section of this book to get Started. There is no such thing as a Time Limit on Connection or the Capability for a Non Physical Human Soul to Connect to a Physical Human after Time.

. . .

When reading this, you may have a Transitioned Loved One who has been in The Ethereal Realm for some Time, perhaps many years. Know that it is ok if you have never been wanting to Try for Fear of the Unknown to Start Now. Know that you have not let your Transitioned Loved One down in any way by not Being Ready to Allow. Know that it could Be the perfect Time for you, Now Knowing what you Know from this book. Now could Be the perfect Time to Move Vibrationally to a Place where you are Ready. But no rush. You don't need to Feel the weight of Expectation.

Also Know, that any Feeling of a 'visit' from them in the past was them Trying to let you Know that it is Possible for you to Connect with them. It doesn't Mean that the only way they can come and Be with you is through their own Soul Determination and they will Show up when they aren't too busy or don't have other more Important things that they are Doing. Know Now that yes, they have got other things to Do in The Ethereal Realm, but they Energetically can also Be with you simultaneously, and they so want to Be. In this Knowing, Allow this to Help you Feel a little Shift within about Letting Go some of the Importance of the Connection and just Allow it to Be a bit more 'normal'.

Perhaps in your Family or circle of friends, Connecting and speaking of these types of things in this way isn't 'normal'. But Ask yourself what is not 'normal' about wanting to Connect with a Non Physical Loved One when you can, especially when they so want to also. It may Be True that friends or Family are not Ready for the conversation with a Transitioned Loved One or they are not wanting to Try themselves, but don't let this Influence you, their Fears Do not Need to Be yours. Don't let anybody else's opinion Stop you from Doing what you Feel is True. Your Transitioned Loved One perhaps is someone that you have never met, perhaps they Transitioned before you became a Physical Human. Yet, they still Love you so, still wish to support and Guide you and Be there for you in any way that you Allow and Need them to Be. In many cases, you will have been together in The Ethereal Realm and their Soul too may have been involved and engaging with you in preparation for you before your Transformation to The Physical Realm . Isn't that the most Wondrous Possibility? Feel into this Now, Feel into the Energy of your Transitioned Loved One that you haven't Connected to yet and Feel if this Feels True to you or the Possibility of it Feels True to you.

"I Feel So Fearful Of Connecting, What Can I Do?"

We completely Understand, so many Feel the same way. Either they have had a previous Experience of Connecting to Non Physical Humans or what they thought was a Non Physical Human, or they have Heard of others' bad Experiences, or they just Find the Concept of it strange and Unknown around what to expect and also what to Do.

With many misnomers around Non Physical Energy and also around 'Protection' from this Energy, so called 'dark Energy' or 'lost Souls', it can Lead to a whole bunch of Fear around even thinking about wanting to Try. So a couple of things to firstly clear up.

We have mentioned already about the Translation of Energy, which is what happens when Receiving Non Physical Energy. You Now Understand that your Transitioned Loved One is Vibrating at a different Frequency to you, and in that Vibration, that Energy Must Be interpreted by you, therefore you Translate with it and Receive it. When you yourself are Feeling Low Vibrational, in other words any Low Vibration Emotion or combination of Emotions such as Grief, Sadness, Fear of Death, Fear of Failure, Fear of the Unknown, loss etc., it can either Stop you from Receiving all together, because there is too much of your own Low Vibration in the way or, if you Do Receive, the Translation of that Non Physical Frequency can become Low Vibrational because of your own Low Vibration. In that Low Vibrational Translation, it is at that point where 'MisTranslation' can occur and in this scenario the Receiving Physical Human Interprets incorrectly based on their own negative Thoughts and Perspectives. Literally any negative Thought can Infiltrate and Influence Translation with Non Physical. For example if the Receiving Physical Human Fears the devil and every Time that they consider Connecting with a Non Physical Human they Trigger their own Subconscious Mind Memories about the devil, it is very possible that when they Receive from the Loving Non Physical Human, that what they will Translate will Be a Sense that they have Connected with the devil. In other words they have completely MisTranslated the actual Loving messages from their Transitioned Loved One as something very negative. Herein lies the Connection to 'dark Energy' or 'evil spirits', it is simply a case of MisTranslation by the Receiving Non Physical Human. There is no devil, no hell, no dark spirit. There are no 'spirits who are lost', or who cannot make their way through Transition. There are no Non Physical Human Souls that are 'between worlds' and Need to Be Freed by a Physical Human. There is only Love, and Loving Non Physical Humans in The Ethereal Realm.

It is Conscious Connection to the Possibility of all of these negative views and Beliefs and Understandings that can in the moment

Create such Confusion for the Receiving Physical Human. For the Influence of a Physical Human, in particular who is Vibrating a lot of Fear, can Be hugely negative. This Means that it is Possible to Feel Fear and have a Fear based Experience even if the Non Physical Human is only bringing you Love, you could, by your own Low Vibration, Influence how you Feel about it and therefore have a Fear Based Experience, even though it wasn't the Truth of that Experience. It makes it True for you. A Transitioned Loved One will Be Vibrating huge Love Energy to you, yet in your Fear, you can Translate that Energy into one of utter Devastation simply because you are Creating the Emotion of Devastation in the moment. That will absolutely Mean that you Interpret the Devastation to Be that of the Loved One you are Receiving from, and therefore Continue to Create a range of Fear Based Perspectives around what you Feel about Being in Non Physical Human Energy.

This is why we speak first and foremost about Ensuring that you are Feeling High Vibrational when looking to Connect with a Loved One, or any Non Physical Human.

The other point that is Important to Understand is that your Transitioned Loved One is not the same Energy as you. What this Means is, you, as you Now Know, have a Unique Energy Signature, making you entirely Energetically Unique. The closest to your own Energy Signature is that of your Higher Self and this is why your Higher Self is the easiest Non Physical Human Soul for you to Connect to. A Transitioned Loved One when Connecting with you, where you Translate and Receive them, may Take a little Time to Tune to and you may Find you can only Do it for short periods of Time before Feeling drained. You Do not Need to Protect yourself from their Energy, but you Do need to Let Go the

Connection when you have finished Translating with them. There are many opinions with regards to Needing to Protect yourself when Connecting with any Non Physical Energy in order to Ensure no harm comes to you. But this is simply not Correct, you will never Be harmed by any Energy from The Ethereal Realm. The only Protection consideration you Need is that of your own Energy drain. So Be mindful to Protect yourself from getting Energetically weakened or tired from any lengthy Interaction with Non Physical Energy. We will explain more on this in the Energetic Enablement Tools Section where we describe how you Go about Connecting to Non Physical Humans.

For those of you that may still have some Uncertainty about this here are some great Truths that you can Create that will Help you to Let Go of some of the Fears that you may Hold around Connection with Non Physical Humans. With all Truths, they Must Be Felt by you, or they are not your Truths, just stated Intention. So, Try some of these and make sure you Feel that they are True when you have said them out loud, or to yourself.

The Truth is I want to Connect to my Transitioned Loved One

The Truth is I Believe that there is only Love for me from Non Physical Humans

The Truth is that Non Physical Humans are Human and not something to Fear

The Truth is the devil Does not Exist

The Truth is I am not Being Judged by anyone in The Ethereal Realm, including God

The Truth is I can choose to Let Go the Connection with a Non Physical Human whenever I want to

The Truth is I will not Be 'Taken over' by any Spiritual Energy

The Truth is I will Recognise when I am Vibrating Fear and will choose to Let Go the Connection

The Truth is I am Ready to Trust Connection to Non Physical Humans

The Truth is I am Free to choose if I want to Do this and nobody is Forcing me to Do it

The Truth is I am not letting anyone down by not wanting to Do this until I am Ready

The Truth Is there is no evil Energy in The Ethereal Realm

The Truth Is I won't Be lied to by my Transitioned Loved One

There are many other Truths that these may Trigger that you may also want to Create. Allow yourself to Settle, there is no rush and there is no Time limit, just Be in a Vibrational Place where you Feel good before you Move onto wanting to Connect. If you struggle to Create these Truths then Follow the 'Believe Releasing Process' as mentioned in the 5th Dimension Earth's book Believe. Your Higher Self will then Help you to Understand what it is that is Stopping you from Creating these Truths.

"What Does My Transitioned Loved One Get Out Of Connecting With Me?"

Every Non Physical Human Soul who has been a Physical Human absolutely Loves to Connect with their Loved Ones that remain in The Physical Realm. They would Love nothing more than for you to Feel what they Feel about Being a Non Physical Human. They would Love for you to Be able to Feel the Clarity that they Now Do, the Broadest Perspective that they Now Allow and have Access to. They would Love nothing more than to Help you when you Need them, by Guiding you in a way that doesn't Take away your 'Free Will' or your right To choose but instead, Helps you to Understand more about what is Possible for you and what you are Capable of. They would Love to Share with you how good it is to Feel Free from Fear and they would Love nothing more than for you to Feel Free From Fear whilst you are still a Physical Human. They would Love to Share with you Energetically who they are becoming, what they are Working towards in The Ethereal Realm, what it could Mean and how incredible it is to Be as they Now are. They would Love you to Feel what they Feel, the utter Love and Connection and Energetic Satisfaction of Being Eternal.

With all of this Love, there is also Energetic Stretching and Expansion for them because of Being able to Connect with you. We have mentioned previously that it Takes a Transitioned Non Physical Human a whole lot of Energy in order to Connect, and Translate with a Physical Human. In Doing so it Energetically can Be Taxing but in a way that is Exercising for their Soul Energy. It can Mean, just by your simple Interactions with them, that they are Being Exercised Exponentially in this Interaction which in turn will bring forth to them new Capability that ordinarily would Take them a lot longer to Enact. You are not Responsible for 'keeping their Energy alive' so please Do not Feel the burden of this, they have more than enough Energy of their own to Do what they want to Do. There are however a significant and incredible range of Possibilities for them that come from Interacting with a Physical Human, so See your Connection with them as a great big Circle Of Love.

I Want To Try...What Do I Need To Do?

Firstly, we are so happy for you and for your Transitioned Loved One. For many of you, to even get to this point of wanting to Connect with a Non Physical Human has Taken a whole lot of Energy and some Letting Go. Feel really good about this and Now really Allow it. This is a great Vibrational Place to Start from.

When you are Ready, Go to the Energetic Enablement Tools and there you will Find the step by step process of how to Connect to your Transitioned Loved One.

21

NOW LIVE KNOWING THAT THEY DO TOO

Allow a moment of Possibility to occur right Now.

Allow yourself to Let Go.

Allow your Loved ones that have Transitioned to Be Free from your Fear for them.

Allow yourself to Be. Be Human.

No words in this book can Change what has happened to your Transitioned Loved One or Loved Ones. No words in this book can Change the fact that if you are a Physical Human, that Transition will occur for you, for some sooner than wanted or expected.

Understanding and Acceptance is what you Need if you Fear Transition, or Fear the Transition of others that you Love, or Fear for those that have already Transitioned.

. . .

Allow your Soul to Lead you to the Knowing of the Truth of this book, of Love after Death, Eternal Life, and God.

Transition is a moment of Glory, for those left behind in The Physical Realm as well as those that Leave it behind. It is a moment that Non Physical Humans Cherish and we Hope that Now, Physical Humans can also. For Transition is a Statement. A Statement of Courage, of Love for The Self, and of your Achievement.

Many Souls when Created choose not to Undertake a Physical Life, for what is Asked of them is something that they Do not wish to Live. If that decision is Taken there is nothing but Love from God and the Higher Self of that Soul, for they have chosen Self Love and this is all that God Asks of All. But for those that decide to Transform to a Physical Human and Live a Physical Life, Know too that this also is a decision of Self Love.

For those that choose to Live a Physical Human Life embark on the most Outstanding Of Journeys. A Journey so full of Possibility, yet a mere blink of an eye in their Eternal Journey. Try to make it full of Self Love, you chose to Be Physical to fill your Journey with it.

For those of you reading this that are currently Undertaking a Physical Human Life.

Remember.

Remember that Soon you will all Be back together. Eternally. Whether you Leave them behind in The Physical Realm or they Leave you.

. . .

It matters not which way around this will Be. We wish only that when your Transition occurs...well...what Do we wish...

We wish that you have Loved as much in your Physical Life as you are Going to Love when you once again Live in The Ethereal Realm as a Non Physical Human.

Let Go Now.

Be Human.

Go Live.

V

ENERGETIC ENABLEMENT TOOLS

22

WHAT ARE ENERGETIC ENABLEMENT TOOLS?

There are countless ways that Physical Humans can Understand, Utilise, Harness, Discover and Know more about Energy. Here are some simple Energetic Enablement Tools that can be Undertaken at any Time in order to Feel that Connection and Know more about what has been Shared in this book by Experiencing it whilst in The Physical Realm.

Every single Physical Human is Capable of Energy Interaction and these Tools Help to provide an easy way to Try, at any Time, to Discover what Feels Good in the moment with some of what has been Understood and Remembered through reading this book.

Understanding The Power of Energetics is part of what 5th Dimension Earth is bringing forth at this Time. For more information about Energetics, Go to www.5thdimensionearth.com for current Programmes and Events.

23

CONNECTING TO A TRANSITIONED LOVED ONE WHO YOU HAVE KNOWN IN YOUR PHYSICAL LIFE

Connecting to a Transitioned Loved One is an Energetic Process. You are Asking for them to come and spend Time with you. It may Be the first Time that you have Consciously Done this. If you Follow the steps below, it will Enable you the best Opportunity for Connection. Remember, your Vibration is really Important, so if you are Forcing this or if you are Fearing, it will limit the chance for you to Connect without MisTranslation.

Step 1: Relax. Breathe. Close your eyes if you want to

Step 2: Set the Intention Now to 'Connect' to your Transitioned Loved One, say their name

Step 3: Feel into a Memory of Being with them whilst they were a Physical Human. A Memory of Love and Happiness and Connection between you

Step 4: Remember and Feel every Interaction, what it was like to Be in their Energy, what did their laugh sound like, what were they wearing, what did they Move like, what did they say, what did it Feel like to have a hug from them

Step 4: Keep Feeling Relaxed and at Ease

Step 5: Now 'Call' your Transitioned Loved one to you (this is an Energetic Ask)

Step 6: You will Feel a Change of Energy around you, you may Experience some tingles or Feel a temperature Change or some pressure in your Head or different parts of your Physical Body. Just keep Allowing Now and Feel Ready to Allow, you can even say to yourself "I'm Ready to Allow"

Step 7: They will Be in a particular Place, just like they are sitting next to you or in front of you. They won't Move around, they will Be Calm and still, so Notice where they are

Step 8: Now, Tune into their Energy. Think of it like a radio station Tuner, you are Focusing upon their Energy and wanting to get that point where you Feel it is as clear as it can Be. Don't think too hard about how to Do this, your Soul 'Knows' so just Set the Intention to Tune to them. In Doing this, you may See their Energy or Feel their Energy or just Know that they are there

Step 9: When you Feel Ready, Ask them to Give you a hug. It will Be a Vibrational hug but you will also Feel your Love Vortex, right in the centre of your Chest Flow and Expand, so a little like a hug from the inside out as well as Feeling their Energy on the outside of your Physical Body

Step 10: Relax, Feel Happy about your Connection and like you are Settling down for a quick conversation with them. Remember, there is no limit to how many Times you can Connect with them, so Take it slowly and Enjoy any Interaction

Step 11: Ask any question that you want to Ask and Allow yourself to Receive the answer from them. Remember, this answer can come in many forms. You may See, Hear, Feel or just Know what the answer is

Step 12: Continue to speak with them or just Enjoy Being in their company for as long as you want to

Step 13: When you are Ready, Set the Intention to 'Let Go' your Connection with them. You will Feel them Energetically Move away and you will Feel the Connection to them Go for Now

Well done! What was that like for you? How did it Feel? What did you Understand? How Does it Feel to you that you could Do this at any Time? What would you Do differently next Time?

24

CONNECTING TO A TRANSITIONED LOVED ONE WHO YOU HAVEN'T KNOWN IN YOUR PHYSICAL LIFE

This could Be an Ancestor or a friend of the Family that you have Heard others talking about that you would really like to get to Know, or perhaps a Loved One that you met only briefly.

Remember, your Vibration is really Important, so Feel Balanced and Ready.

Step 1: Relax. Breathe. Close your eyes if you want to

Step 2: Set the Intention Now to 'Connect' to your Transitioned Loved One

Step 3: Focus on an image of them in your Mind that you have Seen, perhaps a photo, video or you Energetically remember someone describing them

Step 4: Really Focus in on the image in your Mind, blow it up, make it as big and real as possible, almost like it is animated. Notice all that you can about the image

Step 5: Keep Feeling Relaxed and at Ease

Step 6: Now 'Call' your Transitioned Loved One to you (this is an Energetic Ask)

Step 7: You will Feel a Change of Energy around you, you may Experience some tingles or Feel a temperature Change or some pressure in your Head or different parts of your Physical Body. Just keep Allowing Now and Feel Ready to Allow, you can even say to yourself "I'm Ready to Allow"

Step 8: They will Be in a particular Place, just like they are sitting next to you or in front of you. They won't Move around, they will Be Calm and still, so Notice where they are

Step 9: Now, Tune into their Energy. Think of it like a radio station Tuner, you are Focusing upon their Energy and wanting to get that point where you Feel it is as clear as it can Be. In Doing this, you may See their Energy or Feel their Energy or just Know that they are there

Step 10: When you Feel Ready, Ask them to Give you a hug. It will Be a Vibrational Hug but you will also Feel your Love Vortex, right in the centre of your Chest Flow and Expand, so a little like a hug from the inside out as well as Feeling their Energy on the outside of your Physical Body

Step 11: Relax, Feel happy about your Connection and like you are Settling down for a quick conversation with them. Remember, there is no limit to how many Times you can Connect with them, so Take it slowly and Enjoy any Interaction

Step 12: Ask any question that you want to Ask and Allow yourself to Receive the Answer from them. Remember, this answer can come in many Forms. You may See, Hear, Feel or just Know what the answer is

Step 13: Continue to speak with them or just Enjoy Being in their company for as long as you want to

Step 14: When you are Ready, Set the Intention to 'Let Go' your Connection with them. You will Feel them Energetically Move away and you will Feel the Connection to them Go for Now

Well done! What was that like for you? How did it Feel? What did you Understand? How Does it Feel to you that you could Do this any Time? What would you Do differently next Time?

25

YOUR UNCONSCIOUS GATEWAY

Using your Gateway, which is at the top of your Head and through your Pineal Gland, is the most common approach for Connecting to and Translating with a Loved One, or any other Non Physical Human. To find out more about Your Gateway, please reference the 5th Dimension Earth book Believe.

There is however, another way to Connect. Another Expansive way to Connect to and to Allow Non Physical Connection. This is Connecting using Your Unconscious Gateway, which is in and around your Hope Vortex, which is where your Solar Plexus is. What is your Hope Vortex? Your Hope Vortex is one of the five Vortexes of Emotion that are part of your Inner Being or Soul and it is through your five Vortexes of Emotion that you Create all Emotions as you Go about Living your Physical Human Experience. You can See in the diagram at the end of this section where each of the Vortexes of Emotion are; Trust, Love, Hope, Truth and Strength. Should you wish to Understand more about The Vortexes of Emotion we would recommend that you read 5th

Dimension Earth's book which dedicates a whole chapter to this incredible topic.

Your Unconscious Gateway Flows through your Hope Vortex of Emotion. It is possible for you to Feel into the area of your Solar Plexus and you will Be able to Sense Energy there when you Focus upon it; it will Be your Soul Energy that you Feel and not the Emotion of Hope. The Emotion of Hope is only Felt when it is specifically Triggered by your Vortex of Emotion. The Unconscious Gateway utilises the Hope Vortex of Emotion but when Energy Flows through it the Energetic Feelings you Sense will Be linked to that Energy Type Flowing through it.

Try and Sense Energy Flowing through your Unconscious Gateway Now. Perhaps look at the diagram at the end of this section so you can See where it is fully and Allow yourself to just Feel, you will get an Energetic Response. It may Be subtle, it may Be really strong, but either way, it is there. It could Be a pulsating or a Flow, a flutter of Energy or an Energetic Opening Feeling. When you Feel a Connection to the Energy via The Unconscious Gateway, you will Notice that it spreads. Not all the way through your Physical Body but it reverberates and Expands outwards.

Utilising Your Unconscious Gateway brings you great Expansion, because you are Feeling an Energetic Connection but also you are Allowing less Conscious Mind Influence and Thought as you are Connecting. For so many, using Your Unconscious Gateway for Energetic Interaction also brings really quick Connection, Importantly, to your own Soul Energy. Through this Connection to Your Unconscious Gateway, you can Activate your Connection to your Higher Self, or to a deeper Connection to a Transitioned Loved

One, to another Non Physical Guide or to Feel more of your Soul Energy. We have some Energetic Enablement Tools at the end of this book which will Help you Learn how to Use your Unconscious Gateway in different ways.

The benefit of Using Your Unconscious Gateway is that you can Connect but still Be more Consciously Physical and Present in your Surroundings. It drives more Cognitive Understanding too, so the Feeling and Knowing of your Soul for example and some of the detail we have spoken of relating to the Physical Human Soul Model, you can utilise this Connection in order to Cognitively Receive more and more about your own Energy. As you evolve this and as you wish to Try more types of Connection, you can extend this to your Higher Self or a Connection to the Chamber Of God for example.

What happens is, over Time, the more you Use your Unconscious Gateway, the automatic Connection to your Soul Energy will Start to occur, you just Need to Set the Intention and you Feel it.

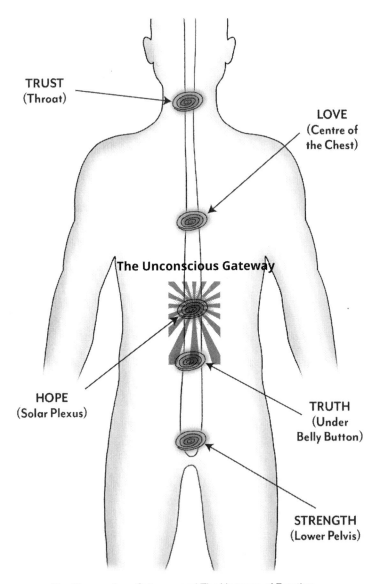

The Unconscious Gateway and The Vortexes of Emotion

26

FEEL YOUR SOUL ENERGY

As you Now Understand where Your Unconscious Gateway is, you are Now able to Use it. This is Intention based, just like all Energetic Connection. You have complete Control with what you Allow and how often you Use this Connection. You are able to Stop at any Time, simply by Intending to 'Let Go' the Connection.

So, why not Feel into your Soul Energy, it is a great Place to Start for it is yours. As you Now Know, you are utterly Unique. Never before has a Soul Energy been Created quite like yours, and yours has also evolved since you have been Physically Human.

Follow these steps in order to Feel your Soul Energy:

Step 1: Relax and Let Go any tension that you are Feeling, in particular in your diaphragm and Solar Plexus area

Step 2: Set the Intention to Feel your Soul Energy

Step 3: Feel your Unconscious Gateway Trigger and Energetically Open. Remember, this is where your Hope Vortex is, right in your

Solar Plexus and the Energy will Feel like it disperses outwards as you Connect to it

Step 4: Flow inwards through your Unconscious Gateway and you will reach your Soul Energy. Once you Feel the Connection, you will Feel the fullness of your Soul as the Connection Flows from the Connection point at your Unconscious Gateway, then runs downwards towards the base of your Pelvis and upwards through your Chest, Throat and Head to your Pineal Gland. If you are unsure, we would suggest it may Help to read the Chapter on The Physical Placement of your Soul

Step 5: Now you are Connected fully to your Soul Energy, Feel the different Flow of it, for it is never static and in situ, it is Energetically in motion. In this Feeling, you can also Zone into some of the different Elements of The Soul Energy that we have spoken of within this book in order to Feel them as distinct Energies. Don't worry if you can't Do this just yet, what is most Important is that you just are able to Connect to your Soul Energy and Feel it's Flow

Step 6: Really just Enjoy the Feeling, so Relax into it, Hold the Connection for as long as you can. You won't Be Energetically drained by it, in fact it will Feel uplifting, but as you are Starting out with this type of Connection, the Conscious Focus is the thing that may make you Feel a little drained, but over Time it will Feel like second nature to you

Step 7: When you are Ready, you can just Intend to 'Let Go' the Connection and you will Feel the Energetic Release from your Soul Flow of Energy and you will get a Sense that the Energy Flow is outwards through Your Unconscious Gateway

27

IGNITE YOUR ETERNAL LIFE FLOW

You will Now Understand through reading the Chapter about the Earth Bound Physical Human Soul Model that part of the inherent makeup of your Soul is your Eternal Life Flow. To Be able to Connect to it and indeed Ignite it provides a Wondrous Feeling in the moment but then also Gives you the Opportunity to Create broader Connection Opportunities.

Step 1: Relax and Let Go any tension that you are Feeling, in particular in your diaphragm and Solar Plexus area

Step 2: Set the Intention to first Feel your Soul Energy

Step 3: Feel your Unconscious Gateway Trigger and Energetically Open. Remember, this is where your Hope Vortex is, right in your Solar Plexus and the Energy will Feel like it disperses outwards as you Connect to it

Step 4: Flow inwards through your Unconscious Gateway and you will reach your Soul Energy. Once you Feel the Connection, you will Feel the fullness of your Soul as the Connection Flows from the Connection point at your Unconscious Gateway, then runs downwards towards the base of your Pelvis and upwards through your Chest, Throat and Head to your Pineal Gland. If you are unsure, please re-read the Chapter on The Physical Placement of your Soul

Step 5: On Feeling the Flow of your Soul Energy, Set the Intention to 'Ignite' your Eternal Life Flow. You will Feel a Shift in your Soul Flow Energy. You may Feel a distinction of the Eternal Life Flow, almost like it is Being highlighted

Step 6: Hold your Eternal Life Flow Ignition for a while and get Used to the Feeling and sensation of it. You will Feel that it Flows through the top of your Head also, so See how far you can Follow it

Step 7: Zoom in on the Feeling of the Eternal Life Flow within the centre of your Physical Body. You may Start to Feel a different Flow to your broader Soul Energy. You may Start to See a Colour, or flecks of Colour Energy if you are able to Translate by Seeing. If not, just remain Focused on the Feeling of it

Step 8: When you are Ready, you Set the Intention to Let Go the Connection to your Eternal Life Flow. You can Continue to Feel into your Soul Energy if you wish to, or Let Go the Connection altogether

28

CONNECT WITH YOUR HIGHER SELF THROUGH THE UNCONSCIOUS GATEWAY

The Higher Self is discussed in detail within the 5th Dimension Earth book Believe. There is also a Free Higher Self Programme available to All on the 5th Dimension Earth Website which explains in detail all about The Higher Self and how you can Tune to them and Connect to them. At this point, if you are unsure about who or what a Higher Self is, we Encourage you to Find out more through these avenues before Connecting, just to Ensure your Understanding.

If you are completely Understanding the concept of a Higher Self and are ready to Try a new way to Connect to them, just Follow these simple Steps:

Step 1: Relax and Let Go any tension that you are Feeling, in particular in your diaphragm and Solar Plexus area

Step 2: Set the Intention to first Feel your Soul Energy

Step 3: Feel your Unconscious Gateway Trigger and Energetically Open. Remember, this is where your Hope Vortex is, right in your Solar Plexus and the Energy will Feel like it disperses outwards as you Connect to it

Step 4: Flow inwards through your Unconscious Gateway and you will reach your Soul Energy. Once you Feel the Connection, you will Feel the fullness of your Soul Energy as the Connection Flows from the Connection point at your Unconscious Gateway, then runs downwards towards the base of your Pelvis and upwards through your Chest, Throat and Head to your Pineal Gland. If you are unsure, please re-read the Chapter on The Physical Placement of your Soul

Step 5: On Feeling the Flow of your Soul Energy, Set the Intention to 'Ignite' your Eternal Life Flow. You will Feel a Shift in your Soul Flow Energy. You may Feel a distinction of the Eternal Life Flow, almost like it is Being highlighted

Step 6: Hold your Eternal Life Flow Ignition for a while and get Used to the Feeling and sensation of it

Step 7: Ask your Higher Self to Be with you Now. You will Feel a Flow of Energy through your Soul as your Higher Self's Energy 'Weaves' with yours. This is a Wondrous Feeling of Connection, so really just Allow it to Be and Feel as much as you can. Keep Allowing if you Feel that you are Denying the Connection

Step 8: You will Feel your Higher Self both Energetically within and external to you Now. You can Ask questions of them, or just home in on their Energy. They will Be Sharing Love with you, so you will Feel a Loving Feeling spread through your Chest and also Hope will Be Triggered by them. If you find a tightness or a blocking sensation in your Throat, this is an Opportunity for you to Trust your Connection with them, so just Allow a little more and this will Ease

Step 9: Spend as much Time as you have or wish to with them. Enjoy the Experience, your Soul will Feel Expanded after this Interaction

Step 10: When you are Ready, Let Go the Connection. You will Feel your Soul Energy Flow Change, you will Feel your Higher Self's Energy Retraction and you will then Feel your Disconnection from Your Unconscious Gateway

29

VISIT THE CHAMBER OF GOD

In this Connection, you are Accessing your Soul's Energetic Holding within the Chamber Of God. Everyone has one! As has been explained earlier in the book, this is a Unique Energetic Holding for you to spend Time in, both as a Physical Human and Non Physical Human. Over Time and as you evolve if you so Desire it, you can Use this Connection to Enable more exploration of your Abilities and Capabilities, and to Work with your Higher Self on specific Intentions or to Receive from your Higher Self in a more deliberate and Conscious way.

Before you Start, it is really good just to Feel into the Intention to See what it is like and Be as Open as you Possibly can to Experience whatever you Experience. Try to not put too much pressure on yourself about it Being a profound Experience and one that is of great Importance. By just Being Relaxed and at Ease about it, you are Going to put yourself Vibrationally into a good Place to Enjoy the Experience. For it should Be Enjoyable! Expansive yes, different yes, but definitely Enjoyable.

. . .

Step 1: Relax and Let Go any tension that you are Feeling, in particular in your diaphragm and Solar Plexus area

Step 2: Set the Intention to first Feel your Soul Energy

Step 3: Feel your Unconscious Gateway Trigger and Energetically Open. Remember, this is where your Hope Vortex is, right in your Solar Plexus and the Energy will Feel like it disperses outwards as you Connect to it

Step 4: Flow inwards through your Unconscious Gateway and you will reach your Soul Energy. Once you Feel the Connection, you will Feel the fullness of your Soul as the Connection Flows from the Connection point at your Unconscious Gateway, then runs downwards towards the base of your Pelvis and upwards through your Chest, Throat and Head to your Pineal Gland. If you are unsure, please re-read the Chapter on The Physical Placement of your Soul

Step 5: On Feeling the Flow of your Soul Energy, Set the Intention to 'Ignite' your Eternal Life Flow. You will Feel a Shift in your Soul Flow Energy. You may Feel a distinction of the Eternal Life Flow, almost like it is Being highlighted

Step 6: Hold your Eternal Life Flow Ignition for a while and get Used to the Feeling and sensation of it

Step 7: Set the Intention to 'Go' to your Energetic Holding in the Chamber Of God. In Enacting 'Go' you will Energetically Move and 'Stretch' via your Eternal Life Flow to your Energetic Holding in The Chamber Of God. Your Soul is not leaving your Physical Body, nor is it Activating The Christ Consciousness Gateway. You are simply Expanding your Soul Energy Interaction Consciously to Connect to a point within The Chamber Of God that Holds your Energy Signature. This Means it is always Possible for you to Energetically spend Time there

Step 8: When you are in your Energetic Holding you may Feel, See, Hear or just Know more about it. For example, what imagery Do you See or Feel as part of the location? What Emotions Do you Feel Being here? What is it that you can Start to Sense or Know about your own Soul? You can Flow with this, Allow yourself to Feel, See, Hear or Know whatever you wish to whilst you are here

Step 9: Be mindful of your Energy, Notice if you Start to Feel a little drained. If you have Understood what you wanted to and it Feels Good to you, you can 'Let Go' the Connection and in Doing so you will Feel your Soul Energy Flow from The Chamber Of God, Flow back to your Soul within your Physical Body and then your Energy Releasing from Your Unconscious Gateway

30

CONNECT TO YOUR EMOTIONAL SIGNATURE

This is a great one to Try after you have Used Your Unconscious Gateway to Connect with your Higher Self. You will Need your Higher Self Engaged in this Energetics Tool in order to Receive the detail that you Need relating to your Emotional Signature. Your Emotional Signature is part of your Soul Energy makeup and there are literally hundreds of different Possible Emotions.

For example, Olivia's Emotional Signature is Magic, which is Strength + Hope. Magic is indeed an Emotion, and if you Trigger your Strength Vortex of Emotion (which is in the lower part of your Pelvis, near the end of your Inner Being/Soul Energy) and Hope Vortex of Emotion (which is in your Solar Plexus, where Your Unconscious Gateway is) you will Feel what Magic Feels like as an Emotion.

Raf's Emotional Signature is Power, which is normally Love + Strength, however his is Strength + Love which provides an emphasis on the Emotion of Strength whilst still Feeling the Emotion of Power. Power is an Emotion that you can Feel, if you Trigger your Love Vortex of Emotion (which is in the centre of your Chest where your sternum is) and your Strength Vortex of Emotion, you will Generate the Emotion of Power.

You can refer to the diagram detailed in The Unconscious Gateway section for Energetic Enablement Tools in order to Understand the Vortexes of Emotion Placement. It Helps to Feel your way through this particular Energetic Enablement and it may Take a few attempts to Be successful, but it is worth the wait and perseverance. You can Feel each Vortex of Emotion one at a Time, Starting with Trust, then Love, Hope, Truth and finally Strength. When all five Vortexes of Emotion are Ignited you Create the Emotion of Faith. You can Find out more about the Vortexes of Emotion and how you Create Emotion by reading 5th Dimension Earth's book Believe.

The other part of this Energetic Enablement is to Try and not Consciously get in the way of what you are Understanding. It is easy for us to Try and 'think' of what our Emotional Signature 'must' Be, based on our Perspective of our Life Experience Interactions but to Be absolutely Correct Follow the steps in this chapter. By Following the instructions and Allowing it to Be True Energy, you will Receive something that when you Feel it, Know it, Understand it to Be True, will Be absolutely Wondrous for you. For once you have Understood your Emotional Signature, you can Use it. Use it in your every day Life. Notice if you are Feeling the opposite of it and Energetically Connect and 'Call' it into your Physical Body from your Soul. It is a great Tool for Vibrational Management!

. . .

Also, just to reconfirm for anyone who is not sure, your Emotional Signature will never Be a negative Low Vibration Emotion, no matter how you are Feeling right Now. It will only ever Be a positive High Vibrational Emotion.

So, how Do you Find out your Emotional Signature? Follow the Steps below:

Step 1: Relax and Let Go any tension that you are Feeling, in particular in your diaphragm and Solar Plexus area

Step 2: Set the Intention to first Feel your Soul Energy

Step 3: Feel Your Unconscious Gateway Trigger and Energetically Open. Remember, this is where your Hope Vortex is, right in your Solar Plexus and the Energy will Feel like it disperses outwards as you Connect to it

Step 4: Flow inwards through Your Unconscious Gateway and you will reach your Soul Energy. Once you Feel the Connection, you will Feel the fullness of your Soul Energy as the Connection Flows from the Connection point at your Unconscious Gateway, then runs downwards towards the base of your Pelvis and upwards through your Chest, Throat and Head to your Pineal Gland. If you are unsure, please re-read the Chapter on The Physical Placement of your Soul

Step 5: On Feeling the Flow of your Soul Energy, Set the Intention to 'Ignite' your Eternal Life Flow. You will Feel a Shift in your Soul Flow Energy. You may Feel a distinction of the Eternal Life Flow, almost like it is Being highlighted

Step 6: Hold your Eternal Life Flow Ignition for a while and get Used to the Feeling and sensation of it

Step 7: Ask your Higher Self to Be with you Now. You will Feel a Flow of Energy through your Soul as your Higher Self's Energy 'Weaves' with yours. This is a Wondrous Feeling of Connection, so really just Allow it to Be and Feel as much as you can. Keep Allowing if you Feel that you are Denying the Connection

Step 8: You will Feel your Higher Self both within and external to your Physical Body Now. You can Ask questions of them, or just Focus in on their Energy. They will Be Sharing Love with you, so you will Feel a Loving Feeling spread through your Chest and also Hope will Be Triggered by them. If you Find a tightness or a blocking sensation in your Throat, this is an Opportunity for you to Trust your Connection with them, so just Allow a little more and this will Ease

Step 9: Set the Intention for your Higher Self to Help you Understand your Emotional Signature. You can start by Asking them to Create the Emotion within you so you can Feel it. For some, your Higher Self may 'Send' you the Emotion Name so you can 'See' it. For some, you may Hear your Higher Self say it. For others, you may just Know what it is through a Cognitive Receiving from your Higher Self

Step 10: Does this Feel True to you? You don't Need to decide Now, but if it doesn't quite Feel right, it may have a little more complexity to it, so Feel Free to Ask your Higher Self to Do it for you again or to explain a little more. If you aren't Receiving a lot from them at this stage, that is ok too, just Relax and Know that it may Take a few attempts, but that you are Doing great and your Higher Self thinks so too

Step 11: Ask your Higher Self how else you can Use your Emotional Signature to Help you and Allow them to answer

Step 12: When you are Ready, 'Let Go' your Connection with your Higher Self and in Doing so, you will Feel their Energy Retract

and you will also Feel yourself Disconnect from your Unconscious
Gateway

31

UNDERSTAND YOUR SOUL ENERGY COLOUR

Soul Energy Colour can Be any Colour on the spectrum and can also incorporate Elements or Designs of Colour, so Accents and Hues and Flecks with Light Attributes can Sparkle or Light up. Colour can Be Seen or Felt or Known. This is another really good one to Do once you have Used Your Unconscious Gateway to Connect to your Higher Self and have tried to Understand your Energetic Signature.

Step 1: Relax and Let Go any tension that you are Feeling, in particular in your diaphragm and Solar Plexus area

Step 2: Set the Intention to first Feel your Soul Energy

Step 3: Feel Your Unconscious Gateway Trigger and Energetically Open. Remember, this is where your Hope Vortex is, right in your Solar Plexus and the Energy will Feel like it disperses outwards as you Connect to it

Step 4: Flow inwards through Your Unconscious Gateway and you will reach your Soul Energy. Once you Feel the Connection, you will Feel the fullness of your Soul Energy as the Connection Flows from the Connection point at your Unconscious Gateway, then runs downwards towards the base of your Pelvis and upwards through your Chest, Throat and Head to your Pineal Gland. If you are unsure, please re-read the Chapter on The Physical Placement of your Soul

Step 5: On Feeling the Flow of your Soul Energy, Set the Intention to 'Ignite' your Eternal Life Flow. You will Feel a Shift in your Soul Flow Energy. You may Feel a distinction of the Eternal Life Flow, almost like it is Being highlighted

Step 6: Hold your Eternal Life Flow Ignition for a while and get Used to the Feeling and sensation of it

Step 7: Ask your Higher Self to Be with you Now. You will Feel a Flow of Energy through your Soul as your Higher Self's Energy 'Weaves' with yours. This is a Wondrous Feeling of Connection, so really just Allow it to Be and Feel as much as you can. Keep Allowing if you Feel that you are Denying the Connection

Step 8: You will Feel your Higher Self both within and external to your Physical Body Now. You can Ask questions of them, or just Focus in on their Energy. They will Be Sharing Love with you, so you will Feel a Loving Feeling spread through your Chest and also Hope will Be Triggered by them. If you Find a tightness or a blocking sensation in your Throat, this is an Opportunity for you to Trust your Connection with them, so just Allow a little more and this will Ease

Step 9: Set the Intention Now for your Higher Self to Help you Understand your Soul Energy Colour. You may Feel your Soul Energy Flow slightly Change in Recognition of the Ask.

Step 10: Your Higher Self will Now Flow to you Understanding. You may See it, the Colour or Aspects of it or the word or words of the Colour and any Aspects. You may Feel it or Know it or you may Hear your Higher Self say it to you. Whichever it is, Allow it to Flow to you and stay in that Allowing Energy. Try not to Consciously get in the way, by doubting or Denying it.

Step 11: Once you Feel you have Anchored to The Soul Energy Colour and any detailing that is coming to you, Ask your Higher Self ways that you can Use this Understanding and how you can Use your Soul Energy Colour and Allow them to answer

Step 12: When you are Ready, you can 'Let Go' the Connection with your Higher Self and you will Feel the Disconnection from Your Unconscious Gateway

32

PUSH AND PULL YOUR 'NATURE'

Your Nature is a Unique Element in your Soul, so linked to the Nature Energy of God. Your Nature Pulls in and Pushes out from your Soul Energy, and Shares itself with you and others, regardless of whether you Pull or Push.

Your Nature runs through your Soul Energy so Allow yourself to Live in its continual Pull and Push. The Push is from within. Pushing Your Nature you will Sense the Energy Flowing out of your Solar Plexus but also within you circling around your Soul perpetually.

Pulling Your Nature is from within your Soul. However it will Feel like the Energy is Being pulled through your Solar Plexus towards your Soul, but also at the same Time the Energy will Feel like it is circling around your Soul, from the back to the front, perpetually.

. . .

Pushing Your Nature is also from within your Soul. However it will Feel like the Energy is Being pushed out through your Solar Plexus, but also at the same Time the Energy will Feel like it is circling around your Soul, this Time from the front to the back, perpetually.

Know that Your Nature Pull and Push is Powerful. Know that both Transform your Fear. Try Pulling and Pushing Your Nature any Time that you Connect with a Transitioned Love One or another Non Physical Human as this will dramatically improve Translation with them.

For those of you that say that I cannot Do this...You have not met Your Nature.

Feel Your Nature Now, let it Start to Transform Fear for you.

As you Push Your Nature out through your Solar Plexus, Feel how it circles around your Soul.

'Share' Your Nature with others and Feel how you come back together.

As you Pull Your Nature, Sense it Flowing from your Solar Plexus, Feel how it circles around your Soul once again

'Share' Your Nature with others and Feel how you come back and around together.

Your Nature Does this perpetually with others, and they with you, as you Hold the Intention to Do so.

· · ·

This is the first Time that this information has ever been formally published and that Physical Humans will have been able to Understand the concept of Nature in their Soul Energy and how to Wield it.

Use this new Understanding to Flow away from Fear when Connecting with Non Physical Humans, but also Use this to Flow away from your Fears. When Wielding it, don't just Focus it on individual things or Experiences or people. Focus within. On your Wondrous Self. On your Journey, your Purpose, your Intention and Understanding and your Meaning. On everything you have come to Understand by reading this book. On the Hope and Possibility that it Means for you as you Continue to Live your Physical Life.

Push and Pull Your Nature to 'All'. Feel it Flowing around your Soul Energy.

Start to integrate yourself into who you Truly are so that you, and all around you Feels and Knows it.

ABOUT THE AUTHORS

Olivia and Raf Ocaña are Creators of 5th Dimension Earth, Energy Experts, Spiritual Changemakers, Influencers, Authors, Energetic Healers, Vibrational Masters and Speakers.

5th Dimensional Living Means the raising of the Earth's Vibration by Starting with You First, always with you. It Means Remembering how to Feel and that we want to Feel Good, not Feel full of Fear. To Remember how to choose Love over Fear in each moment. To Remember that we are All Unique, every single one of us and that each person is that Important. To Remember that we are All here for a Purpose and Meaning, therefore we each Have Reason for Being and that we are here to Create and Co-Create with God and with others as part of that Reason.

Olivia and Raf Teach that we as Physical Humans are here to evolve, to Live this incredible Life fully and in order to Do this and in order to Create Change we Must first Let Go the negative of 'What Was' in order to Truly Live Now and Future Focussed. They Teach that Nature is part of Us and we are part of Nature and therefore we Must evolve further to Ensure the Return to this Connection. They Teach that we each have incredible Energetic Abilities within our Soul Energy that can Create so much Wonder, Magic, Transformation, Hope and Freedom, and that we are full of Limitless Possibility. They Teach that we as Physical and Non

Physical Humans want to Share this with others, that we Love Being part of a Community.

Olivia and Raf Work closely with their broader Non Physical Team 'The Abraham and Jesus Collective', to Share Leading Edge Insight and Transformational Change Possibility through their Teachings. Without Connection to their Non Physical Team, they could not Understand or Share the Insight that they are bringing forth at this Time. The Abraham and Jesus Collective is a Powerful and growing Collective and the original members include The Souls of Olivia, Raf, Archangel Adam, Archangel Ophelia, Abraham, Jesus, God and Shala.

Note that you too have a broader Non Physical Team supporting you, it's just that you may not Know it yet or Do not Recognise them when they are around.

The foundation of a 5th Dimension Earth is the Connection and Understanding of The Higher Self, that we each have one, that they are our Connection to the Universe and the Multiverses, and that they are Accessible, Available, and so willing to Help support and Guide us. Olivia and Raf are the World Leading Experts on Connection to your Higher Self and have Created a Free Programme for All who are interested. Just access it by visiting www.5thdimensionearth.com

OTHER BOOKS FROM 5TH DIMENSION EARTH

Believe

25 Messages From Heaven

Printed in Great Britain
by Amazon